At Home in the Park

At Home in the Park

✦

Loving a Neighborhood Back to Life

Lola L. Lucas

iUniverse, Inc.
New York Lincoln Shanghai

At Home in the Park
Loving a Neighborhood Back to Life

iUniverse books may be ordered through booksellers or by contacting:

iUniverse
2021 Pine Lake Road, Suite 100
Lincoln, NE 68512
www.iuniverse.com
1-800-Authors (1-800-288-4677)

ISBN-13: 978-0-595-36482-4 (pbk)
ISBN-13: 978-0-595-67380-3 (cloth)
ISBN-13: 978-0-595-80915-8 (ebk)
ISBN-10: 0-595-36482-9 (pbk)
ISBN-10: 0-595-67380-5 (cloth)
ISBN-10: 0-595-80915-4 (ebk)

Printed in the United States of America

This book is dedicated to my parents, Pauline and Hal Cameron, with thanks for their encouragement not just as parents but as writers themselves.

"All that I am or ever hope to be, I owe to my angel mother."

Abraham Lincoln

We shape our dwellings, and afterwards our dwellings shape us.
—Winston Churchill

Contents

DÉCOR AND ARCHITECTURE

HOLIDAYS

TRAVEL

HUSBAND AND HOUNDS

LOLA'S WORLD

APPENDIX

ACKNOWLEDGEMENTS

THE
ENOS PARK BANNER

I've tried to recall just how it came about to have Lola Lucas write her column for our newsletter, *The Banner*. Had I seen some of her work? I don't remember. I was trying to find interesting things that would be a benefit to the residents of Enos Park. Several people offered suggestions about different subjects. However it came about, it is certainly a gift to all of us to have Lola's writings each month. How lucky we are to have her and her talent for appealing to everyone! I'm sure you will love the book as much as I have enjoyed typing the columns as they've arrived each month for over a decade.

Marilyn R. Piland
Executive Director
Enos Park Neighborhood Improvement Association
Editor of *The Banner*

Introduction

"Love makes us Real."

That's the whole point of *The Velveteen Rabbit*. The Skin Horse says, "Generally, by the time you are Real, most of your hair has been loved off, and your eyes drop out and you get loose in your joints and very shabby. But these things don't matter at all, because once you are Real you can't be ugly, except to people who don't understand."

Neighborhoods are more than a collection of houses. They're a living entity that's a sum of the people who live in them. Like people, they can have good times or bad, booms and busts. They can also fall into despair and depression, going into a negative spiral if their residents lose faith in them. Sociologists developed the "broken window" thesis to explain how physical neglect can lead to a perception of decay followed by withdrawal by the residents, less willingness to intervene to prevent crime, and an influx of outsiders who think the area is a great place for criminal behavior. That's what happened to Enos Park. Like so many urban areas, it fell on hard times. It went from elegant mansions (after all, it was at the Edwards' house that Lincoln courted Mary Todd) and tidy working class homes to a haven for drug dealers. Once-grand buildings were cut up into apartments and litter blew in the alleys. It would've been easy to give up on it and let it continue its slide from neighborhood to slum.

That's not what happened. A group of people decided to see beyond the shabbiness and to take their homes back. Fletcher (Bud) Farrar, Andy Anderson and a host of other investors bought houses and rehabbed them for themselves and for rent or sale. The Enos Park Neighborhood Improvement Association, under the able direction of Marilyn Piland, has spearheaded a variety of events and programs to change first the perception and then the reality of the area. The Spring Festival, the Party in the Park, ice cream socials, citizen patrols and, of course, EPNIA monthly meetings bring residents together to enjoy each other's company. The bonds of community have been re-knit and it's a neighborhood well on the mend. Property values have gone up and crime has gone down. It's a good place to live again.

Like Marilyn, I've forgotten exactly how it was that I began writing columns for our monthly newsletter. I'd moved to Springfield July 4, 1991 from St. Louis and I was lonely, I remember that—I'd left a house I loved, my family, friends and job all to move off to the wilds of Central Illinois. I was trying to find a new community and since I'd owned a house on the National Register and had been active in the University City Historical Society, I read the *Banner* that was stuck in my front door. My newlywed husband Kevin and I began attending the monthly meetings and we both served on the board of directors at various points. We quickly made new friends, too. Believe me, involvement is the sovereign remedy for loneliness.

My first column in the fall of 1992 was about fireplace safety. That was a bit ironic since our house on 4th Street had two fireplaces but neither was functional. Ah, but what a delight they were to look at! Ornate carving, tile work and mirrors, there was one in the parlor and another in the dining room. Like the brass hardware and intricate light fixtures that were original to the house, they were truly the sort of things you can't buy anymore except as salvage or as very expensive reproductions.

As the years went by we watched our neighborhood return to life through a combination of community policing and sheer determination on the part of residents. In the columns that follow you'll see a recurring theme that nothing substitutes for the gritty reality of picking up trash, repairing that broken window and demanding that the junked car be removed. It would've been easier to let Enos Park go but we loved it back to life, house tour by holiday bazaar, bake sale by music event, festivals by free paint giveaways. We feel at home again instead of besieged behind closed doors. We have a lot to be proud of these days.

Like many other Springfieldians, Kevin and I both work for the State of Illinois, he as a programmer/analyst and I as a research economist. My day job involves watching trends that affect economic development, workforce planning and the new technologies creating and eliminating jobs. Much as I enjoy it, all of that take place at a macro level. Yet I started as a career counselor so I find I still care about what happens to individual people and their families. I've had a ringside seat for observing how communities can decline and rebound all across the country and it always comes back to somebody being willing to *do* something.

In a literal sense, Enos Park is an area of Springfield, Illinois that's just a bit north of downtown and the new Abraham Lincoln Presidential Library and Museum. It's bounded by Carpenter, 3rd Street, North Grand and 9th Street. There are houses over a century old and new condominium complexes, local businesses and national chains, schools, churches, restaurants, medical offices and art galleries. But in a broader sense, Enos Park could be anywhere that's facing a choice between decay and renewal. Just like the valuation of stock, there's an element of investor confidence. Can you bet on your own area? Are you willing to risk investing your time and energy to create genuine community instead of just a collection of houses? "Love makes us Real." That's true of toys, people, houses—and neighborhoods. We've loved Enos Park back to life and my wish for you is that you'll join with others to do the same for where you live, too.

Lola L. Lucas
March, 2005

Note: I grouped the columns by topic rather than putting them in chronological order. For the record, we bought 1026 N. 4th Street in 1991 and lived there for three years. We then moved to the Washington Park area of Springfield and kept the house as rental property for another seven years.

(It won the Mayor's Award for Historic Preservation in 2001.) Kevin and I have remained involved with EPNIA because they're some of the most delightful people we've ever met.

~ENOS PARK~

Snapshots of the Heart

"Memories are the snapshots of the heart."

The morning is cool and overcast so I'm glad that Kevin brought his windbreaker. We anxiously scan the sky but while the sun hides, at least it doesn't rain. The originally scheduled date in May had been a swamp, with Enos Park ankle deep in mud from a week of downpours. Now in June it's drier and the plans for the Party in the Park proceed. Deb's got the set-up under control so we actually even have time to go for some coffee. We return with a pleasant caffeine buzz and get settled in at our table to sell tickets for the food and games at 25 cents each. *Click.*

A clown makes clever designs from balloons for children who crowd around her at the edge of the playground. She stops by our table while waiting for a replacement balloon pump to arrive. Turns out she used to be a rodeo clown and this is the first time she's performed in public for 15 years. "Bulls were easier than the kids," she laughs. Later, she'll get dizzy from blowing soap bubbles all around the park. *Click.*

Kevin buys a single ticket for me and I traipse over to the fortune teller. She's in a long flowing gray dress with an elaborate purple turban. Her hands are covered in rings and she drips with jewelry. I introduce myself then feel quite silly—it's Leona; I've known her for years and admired her ramrodding of the neighborhood patrol. But she looks different when she's talking about getting crime off the streets. Now her face has a relaxed and open kindness that makes me think of Mother Nature herself. She peers at my hand. "Ah, a long life line," she announces. Her finger touches feathery lines I'd never noticed before. "You have many friends." She doesn't take it seriously and neither do I, but it's a nice chance to chat about my writing and her upholstery and how we envy each other's skills. A little boy comes up and asks in awe, "Are you a psychic?" "Oh, no," she replies. "But I can tell you what *ought* to be in store for your future for someone your age…" She says it with such compassion and love—and with the adult knowledge that what ought to be sometimes isn't how things work out—that I can feel tears starting. So I slide away and let others cluster around to fill her coffee can with tickets. *Click.*

A little girl with her face painted in zebra stripes comes to a stop on her bicycle in front of our table. She wants to buy a few tickets at a time instead of spending her whole $5 at once and we admire her prudence. Yet $5 does go fast after all and her smile as she gives us the last dollar says it's been money well spent. She had a lot of ways to use her tickets: on a trampoline, a moonwalk, hot dogs, cotton candy, and assorted games. Children run all over while parents stroll behind them. Dan and Gayle's solemn wee girl has her face painted like a cat. She stands on the sidewalk, deciding what to do next. *Click.*

Kevin and I talk to the grown-ups and ask them how the neighborhood is these days, whether the association is doing any good. "Well, it used to be our car windows got broken out every year. Our insurance man told us to move away from here. But it's been a year and a half now since the last broken window and we're hoping it'll stay that way." *Click.*

A gentleman with flowing white hair and mustache buys a dollar's worth of tickets for food. He's back in a few minutes to get more. "Those cookies Marilyn made are just *great*," he says fervently. *Click.*

Deb is everywhere, organizing, poking, prodding, making sure the raffle tickets get sold and the prizes awarded. I enjoy the earnest way children and adults guess the number of red hots in a jar to win a $25 gift certificate from Grand Meats. Somehow it seems quaint to guess numbers in a world where computers can instantly calculate such vast sums. Watching our neighbors come out to enjoy the park and the food and the games and each other makes me profoundly pleased. This isn't nostalgia, this is reality. It's community. I admit it, I feel smug comparing Enos Park to the subdivisions on the west side of town. It's something you can't buy—it has to be earned with the hours put in by willing hearts, hands and minds. *Click.*

Memories are snapshots of the heart.

(July 1996)

Ice Cream Social

"I'm just so depressed about turning 30," whined a co-worker. "Do you have a job?" I asked. "One where you're doing interesting projects and learning marketable skills?" Yes. "And you're happily married, right?" Well, yes," again. "And you have friends and family who love you and you're healthy?" All true.

Later, when another co-worker mentioned that she didn't get much sympathy for her birthday angst, I couldn't take it any more. Sure, I've known people who'd get depressed for months before and after their birthdays whereas this woman routinely griped that life had shortchanged her. I managed *not* to say, "You're not getting older, you're getting bitter." But enough is enough. I told her about children I'd known who died young of neuromuscular diseases back when I was a poster girl for MDA, kids who wanted so very much to live, who'd have given anything for even a few of the years she complained of having accumulated. Then there was the Holocaust Memorial in St. Louis where my mother had worked, and the Jews I'd known with tattooed arms. A few weeks ago friends here in Springfield brought over old family photos to scan into digital form—relatives gone, every one of them, into the concentration camps. For that matter, millions of children are now infected with AIDS in Africa and have no hope of seeing their fifth birthdays, much less their 30th. So why should I agree that it's just dreadful to mark another year?

Backing up, I realized that perhaps it wasn't all about just getting older, or watching those proverbial sands accumulate in the bottom of the hourglass. Maybe people aren't upset at still being alive, but at having lived so little. Some are distressed when age markers like The Big Four O arrive and they're not married, as they thought they'd be, or not parents, or not as far along in a career as planned. If that's what they're upset about, then I can muster more empathy for them, along with a good swift kick in the assets to remind them of what all they *do* have going for them. If it's uncomfortable to find that life is passing them by, then hey, it's time to get up and take charge so that they can celebrate the next birthday as a triumph.

I came across a quote by Ernest Fitzgerald: "It is not by accident that the happiest people are those who make a conscious effort to live useful lives. Their happiness, of course, is not a shallow exhilaration where life is one continuous intoxicating party. Rather, their happiness is a deep sense of inner peace that comes when they believe their lives have meaning and that they are making a difference for good in the world."

On June 23rd we had the ice cream social at Gehrmann Park and there were so many people there who fit that description! I could see it shining in their faces as they tended animals in the petting zoo or scooped orange sherbet or sold raffle tickets. Children squealed with delight at the games and people mingled on a scavenger hunt that introduced them to each other. Mayor Hasara joined us, and I suspect she was pleased to see citizens of every age and race joining for fun in the park. Kevin and I wandered around exchanging pleasantries with neighbors and asked each other if all the food was exceptionally good or if the taste was enhanced by being outside with friends. Both, we decided.

The Enos Park Neighborhood Improvement Association has been blessed with talented people who are working to make our area one of the very best that Springfield has to offer. The events this year have been grand and we have more coming, such as the Christmas House Tour. Watching the rebirth of Enos Park makes me think that it's a privilege, indeed, to be alive.

(July 2001)

Putting Your House on the Tour

There's a certain comfort to confiding a dark secret and discovering that your mate shares it. In this case, I finally broke down and admitted it: I have a hard time finding our new house. Each time I drive down the street, I have to *look* for it. Turns out that Kevin has the same problem.

We moved from Enos Park to Washington Park about a year and a half ago and it really is as nice as people seem to think. We like our neighbors a lot even though they're a competitive bunch—who can get out and shovel the neighbors' sidewalks for them the fastest? (Kevin wasn't about to be outdone by the little slip of a girl two houses up who did our walkways and driveway last time so he was out early shoveling the several inches of "flurries" we got.) Of course, we like the big houses and tree-lined streets and having the park itself only a few steps away. But we settled for a plain American four-square house and while it's roomy, it simply doesn't have the character of our blue house in Enos Park. There was never, ever a problem finding our house as we drove up Fourth Street—it gleamed to us like a beacon. Well, truth to tell, it's a prettier house with painted lady detailing, a tiny attic balcony just right for curling up and reading, bay windows and elaborate carved mantels in both the parlor and dining room. The kitchen is big and filled with light. My mother always said it was an enchanted place with a serene and happy feel to it.

Alas, our house in Washington Park may have more prestige, but it has much less personality. We haven't treated it like a living creature the way we did "The Wee Blue Hoose." I *loved* our home in Enos Park just as I passionately adored my black 1983 Thunderbird. For Kevin, it's even more pronounced because the blue house was by far the nicest place he'd ever lived up to that point. Our home now is larger and more elegant with its modern kitchen, but it lacks the architectural detailing that made 4th Street such a joy—the antique doorknobs and light fixtures, for example.

7

One regret I have is that we didn't put the blue house on the Enos Park Fall House Tour while we lived there. While it's true that my dwellings mostly get cleaned when we're about to have a party, they get *really* fixed up for a house tour. It's almost as inspiring for taking care of the nagging little things as putting a house on the market. However, when the tour's over, I get to continue to live there and benefit from my work! (Why do we do that? Why do we all so often wait to fix things until we move and then let other people benefit from them?)

Have you ever considered putting your house on the tour? Maybe you're thinking, naw, it's too much effort, too much expense. Well, you get to enjoy the improvements and it all probably needs doing anyway. But what if someone steals something or "cases the joint" to come back later? This hasn't happened to any house on a Springfield tour. We've never had a problem and neither have any of the other organizations we've talked to about their experiences with tours. Finally you might say, oh, we have such an ordinary house, who'd want to see it? The Enos Park tour is a broad cross-section of all types of dwellings in the area, showcasing not just the architecture but the style of the people who live here. It's a way for us to brag a bit about what we're so proud of—and deservedly so.

If you put your home on the tour, we can help you research your house's history and you'll also receive a framed house portrait, the original from which the brochure drawings are taken. Get a jump start on spring clean-up and fix-up by calling our executive director, Marilyn Piland, and volunteering for this year's tour! You'll end up being glad you did.

(February 1996)

Selling "The Wee Blue Hoose"

"I guess you won't be writing that column of yours anymore," a friend remarked.

"Why wouldn't' I?" What an odd thought!

"Well, you don't own property in Enos Park now," she replied, secure in her logic. And she's right—we sold "the wee blue hoose," as we called it in our faux Scottish accents, the lovely home we'd lived in for the first three years of our marriage. We'd had renters for nearly seven years because we couldn't bear to part with it but when our tenants moved out, it seemed like time to let it go.

I'm not bragging (OK, maybe a little) but we did a couple of things right to get the house sold in barely over a month. First, we asked Linda Maier of Realty Executives to be our agent since she lives across the street—who better to describe the block to potential buyers than someone who'll be their new neighbor? Second, when she made suggestions for improvements, we were quick to take care of the problems. Drat, that awful odor was from the pieces of carpet in the laundry room! Kevin carried them out and it made a big difference immediately. Third, we tried to make the house as attractive as possible for its new owners. The leaded glass window in the kitchen was restored and I put up new curtains. We carried bags down from the attic and I have to admit, I've lived in Illinois for so long that when I found some shoe boxes up there, I *had* to look inside.

We ended as we had begun, with our dear friends the Murphys helping us. The first day we moved in Joe ripped down wallpaper in the kitchen. It was a paisley stripe avocado green, harvest gold and my memory suggests silver Mylar but maybe it wasn't quite that hideous. It came off in great sheets and we laughed as Joe struggled out from under it. The last weekend of fixing up the house found us all back there again, though the girls

11

are a decade older now and able to swarm up ladders like monkeys. We scraped, painted, swept, picked up trash, whacked weeds and made several runs to Noonan's for supplies (Luke suggested another brand of sealer for the basement walls which made spraying a less smelly process. Kevin would occasionally surface from below, wearing his breathing mask, goggles and a new layer of paint speckles.) When we were ready to wrap for the day, we cleaned up as best we could, then headed for the KFC on North Grand for lunch. Not much beats feeling tired but triumphant and celebrating with good friends.

I admit that I didn't just sniffle, I cried the last day Kevin and I worked on the house. I was in the upstairs front bedroom, the one that looks out into the treetops. It had been our family room with our television and computer where we'd curl up on the couch with Justin and Gyre and Lyren. Only Lyren remains now but I felt as though I could almost step through time to be with our good hound and our precious cat once more. Houses hold memories, I believe, and Fourth Street has always seemed like a profoundly happy place.

So, we neither live in Enos Park nor do we own rental property there. We discovered we're not cut out to be landlords and that was a useful lesson. It was time to have someone else move in who would love the house and treasure it as we had. Yet we're still connected by friendships we've made, by a decade of hopes we've had for the area, and by our efforts to make the house a well-tended part of the neighborhood. We've watched property values rise and I'm delighted to give the donation we promised to EPNIA since I'm positive that the association has had a huge impact on property values over the years. (With the Lincoln library going in, I bet we'll eventually kick ourselves for having sold the house too soon.) Besides, we're still residents of Springfield and that's reason enough to stay involved because good communities add up to better cities.

Not write this column anymore? I've been privileged to hold this spot for nine years and I have a sneaking suspicion that all the time I've looked for my calling in life, I've actually been doing it here. I passionately love buildings and I seem incapable of doing anything other than exhorting people to be involved in their neighborhoods. My mother says this last paragraph in my columns is the "altar call" when I try to wrap up my experiences and use them to explain why *you* need to get active in Enos Park. It's a bully pulpit, indeed. And when it comes down to it, ownership may change hands but hearts can stay in residence forever.

(September 2001)

The Heart and Soul of EPNIA

October. Deep, black nights that fall, shadows that creep, ghosts moaning in chill breezes. Horror—but do you want real horror? Something to make your blood run cold? Worse than *Psycho* or *The Exorcist*?

Then imagine *It's a Wonderful Life* set in Enos Park. What if Marilyn Piland had never existed?

The streets are dark with dilapidated buildings swaying together like ancient tombstones. Raunchy, drunken laughter spills from a drug house where unconscious bodies litter the porches. No one cares enough to call the police because that's the usual scene in an area so bombed out, so decayed, that Springfield's given up hope. There's no grass, only trodden mud between piles of trash. What window glass remains is spider webbed with bullet holes. Sullen fires burn in barrels where ragged people cluster for warmth. Junked cars lie overturned in the remnants of the park, stripped of anything useful. Businesses have long since fled the area and the ones that remain are heavily barred with owners who keep guns close at hand at all times.

But it's *not* that way. You can drive the streets of Enos Park in safety, citizens and police work together to be sure of that. You can stroll down sidewalks cloaked in autumn leaves and hear children playing because families live here. Up and down the avenues you can see signs that read "Renovation in Progress" as once grand homes are restored. New townhouses are being built and businesses have open doors and smiling owners to welcome you. Could one woman really make that much of a difference?

Actually, yes. It was my privilege to nominate Marilyn for the Copley First Citizen Award this year. As I write this, I don't know if they'll have the good sense to select her, but she's among the handful of people in Springfield who have had a tremendous impact. It's not just one thing she does, it's year after year of dedication to making our neighborhood a great place to live. It's the scent of the cookies she bakes for the Fall House Tour, the sound of kids squealing with delight at the Spring Festival she helps organize. It's the glitter of lights for the holiday decorating competition that she started. Run your hand over a building that's been tuck pointed or had its siding scraped and repainted. Wherever you turn, what you see owes something to Marilyn's persistence and vision down through decades in Enos Park. Your property value reflects hours of her life that she has given to make this a true community.

Marilyn has firm ideas about the way things should be done and that makes it difficult for her to delegate. Too often she ends up taking on the work herself to make sure it's done up to her standards. But as quibbles go, that's not a big one. I've long since made peace with the idea that when dealing with Marilyn, it really is best to help where possible and then stand back out of her way as she whirlwinds through. She's willing to do an incredible amount of work such as a dozen newsletters a year and attending endless meetings to prod progress along. People call her when they need something. She redirects them to the appropriate city office or sometimes just takes care of it herself.

If Marilyn Piland didn't exist, we'd be up a creek, folks. We don't tell her often enough how much her work has meant to EPNIA and, directly or indirectly, to each of us. We should. She'll appreciate kind words now more than a statue in the park later. Look around you and see if it would be a wonderful life here without her efforts over the years. Sometimes the difference between horror and joy is plain, old-fashioned hard work.

(October 2000)

Music in the Park

There was sultry music with a pounding beat and young females gyrating wildly. I looked around and there were swingers and high flyers, too, and I was surrounded by almost irresistible temptations. No, not a weekend in Las Vegas, but the Music in the Park on August 22nd. Children played happily on the swings or danced along to Elevator Shoe's blend of rock, funk, jazz, reggae, hip hop and trip-hop. Kevin and I were selling tickets for the desserts and ice cream so we had a view of the chocolate bundt, strawberry layer and angel food cakes plus pineapple pie, brownies and more. OK, that's about as decadent as the Enos Park Neighborhood Improvement Association gets, but in this era of carbohydrate Puritanism, it was nearly risqué.

The freezer chest on a flatbed was a great idea for keeping the buckets of ice cream cold and it worked much better than trying to store them on ice. The volunteers served generous scoops of vanilla. Golden late afternoon turned to early evening on the sort of day that if you ordered it from the Sears catalog would be not just the Good or the Better but the Best. Who could've guessed it was State Fair time?

I enjoyed watching people wander in with a variety of seating options such as aluminum chairs with webbing, those folding contraptions with their sling cases, and of course, good old-fashioned blankets for the ground. Some people sat at picnic tables and I was glad to have one of those molded plastic chairs in the pavilion's shadow. Every now and then a brown beech leaf would fall on the ticket table to remind us that yes, summer is on the wane and autumn is about to take center stage.

A concert in the park is a very different experience than one at, say, Sangamon Auditorium. Those are certainly fun in their own way, but often parents who take their children find they spend time trying to keep them from behaving like...well, like children. It was fun to watch a boy dangling upside down on his dad's lap, his bare feet waving with delight. One little girl rode her bike around and around on the grass and no one said, "Stop that! Not here!" It was just fine. Smiling grandparents pushed kids on swings or hovered as they clambered on monkey bars. Teens wandered around in packs, burning off that notorious energy. Some people flopped over on blankets and read, while a couple cuddled on a park bench. I liked seeing the ethnic diversity and the range of ages from pumpkin seats to powered wheelchairs. Everyone seemed to enjoy Elevator Shoe's tunes, although they never did get around to playing a single polka.

There was one young man who really got into the spirit as he capered and whirled to the music. Part of his dance moves involved occasional grabs for his low-slung jeans as he shimmied and gestured for others to join him. With his goatee, how could I not think of Pan with his equally bare torso—although, of course, this fellow was an urban version with tattoos?

For us, it was a homecoming so it was great to hug friends, shake hands and swap stories for a few hours. (The next evening we had supper with some new acquaintances and mentioned the ice cream social at our neighborhood association. Which one? Enos Park, we replied. "Oh! That's the very best one in town, the most active. You've really gotten a lot done over there." We beamed with pride.) Talking with folks we knew from EPNIA reminded us of just how far we'd come over the years as a community. The first time we worked an event a dozen years ago there were folks buying tickets who had problems grasping that four quarters equaled a dollar. On this evening, people had been drawn to the park district's concert from all over town as well as the neighborhood. Some stopped by to share memories of growing up in the area and their pleasure at seeing all the rehabbing that's going on. Well, we're working on it.

And that's the essence of it: we're working hard, but we still find time to relax with friends, family, food and fun. An ice cream social in a park on an August afternoon—that's not just a Norman Rockwell painting, it's better. It's real.

(September 2004)

The House in the Dumpster

There's something very odd about seeing a house in a trash Dumpster.

Early this year, the house catty-cornered from us burned. It was obvious that it was too gutted to restore and it sat, vacant and charred, for months. I put in a call to Marilyn Piland about the need for the doors and windows to be boarded up to prevent curious children from getting inside and harming themselves and voilà! soon the boards were up. Still, for months as I drove by I could see a lonely hassock upside down on the roof of the porch. It looked forlorn, an object abandoned by its former owners.

Neighbors came out on the sidewalks to watch the actual demolition. There was, indeed, something hypnotic about the fastidious way the wrecker took the house apart. The jaws would reach out and tear away a section of wall with years' accumulation of plaster, paint and wallpaper. Inevitably, being the sentimentalist I am, I thought of the lives which had been lived out within its rooms over the past 70 years. That became a moot point as the heavy equipment operator rolled over the boards and bricks to bring down the last of it leaving nothing but concrete steps leading to what had been the foundation.

Kevin walked over to examine it. "What did it look like?" I asked. "Like a big hole in the ground," he replied. He's nothing if not succinct. Yet he's not immune to sharing the feeling I have that houses are almost living beings and he was sad, too.

Don't get me wrong; there are quite a few houses I'd be pleased to see removed. They've gone past the point of restoration and the kindest thing now would be to level them so that something else can be built in their places. This particular house, though, had a lot of potential for being a solid middle-class home. It was a loss to the neighborhood to see the pieces of it scooped up and put into a couple of trash Dumpsters. It'll go into a landfill and perhaps some future archeologist will glean insight into the

20th century from it. Around it will be junk mail, newspapers, cans and bottles that didn't get recycled and thus it will form a stratum of history.

It's just in the nature of things—houses are built and houses are destroyed. This wasn't an issue about preservation in the sense that the Sacred Heart-Griffin chapel or the Bunn warehouse were. This was a simple, garden-variety case of a house that burned. No one is likely to spend the money to duplicate the construction methods or woodwork that was lost so when they're gone, they're gone and Enos Park is a little poorer for it.

Helen Keller said, "Turn your face to the sunshine and you cannot see the shadows," so we'll look forward to all the renovation that's being done and the new developments that keep the area alive and growing. We'll preserve the best of what we have as a heritage to pass on to the future. I'll applaud each neatly done yard, each new porch or paint job. In time, that corner lot will be filled in and will sit waiting for another home, another family.

(July 1994)

"Shame! Come Back!"

"Shame! Shame! Come back!" I feel like crying out as I run down the streets of Enos Park. But the concept of shame is even more elusive than the hero who rode off into the sunset after saving the town in the movie *Shane*. There was a time when shame and pride worked together, two sides of the same coin, to hold communities together. People had standards of behavior and knew what was acceptable and what was not. Actions had to always be weighed against "what will the neighbors think?" Now *there's* an archaic phrase, isn't it? The idea of people *knowing* their neighbors, much less modifying their actions because of them—how quaint.

Granted, people often enjoyed moving away from little towns or tightly knit communities to escape the scrutiny of neighbors. As the saying goes, in a small town everyone knows whose check is good and whose kids aren't. But we don't have bad kids anymore, we just have children who have been victimized by their socioeconomic status and the educational system. There is truth in that: there's no question that challenging schools and real jobs afterwards create a different climate of expectation for kids than a world where their teachers are often overwhelmed, their families have disintegrated around them and even minimum wage jobs can be hard to obtain with their skills. They are no longer responsible for the fabric of society—heck, if they have no stake in it, why *not* cut and destroy and splash graffiti all over that fabric? Why watch others enjoying its warmth if they're left out in the cold?

Let me give a specific example. A former neighbor of ours was commenting on the woman who was attacked and robbed in an alley behind Fourth Street. "Well, what did she expect, carrying a purse like that?" My answer is, she should *expect* to walk safely in her own neighborhood in broad daylight with a purse—or ideally, even at night, in an alley with enough jewelry to make Ivana Trump envious. That's what life *should* be, and, in some cases, *was*, in communities where everyone knew each other and crime was not an act by faceless perpetrators. (I'm not naively nostalgic; I am aware that there was crime in "the good old days" too, but certainly not to this extent and not so often neighbors preying on neighbors.)

Imagine if people were ashamed to even *think* of stealing from others, be it mugging, burglary, carjacking or vandalism. What if families, schools, churches, celebrities and the media all uniformly and consistently showed that violence was shameful? What if sin was having a baby that one couldn't support, whether within wedlock or out of it? There was a time when being a drug addict was a shameful thing, not a source of endless government assistance on disability payments. I understand that addiction is a disease process but I think that, at one time, community standards kept most kids from ever taking the first hit of a drug.

The flip side of shame is pride. Kids could strive not just for some sort of nebulous self-esteem concepts, but self-respect based on pride for hard work, pride for a job well done. I make a point of tearing articles out of the paper that show how children today can get involved in positive groups that help them learn to take their place as the leaders of society. What do kids want? They're human beings so they want what all of us want: time and attention. They can get it in scout troops better than in juvenile courts. To a child, any attention is better than none. Isn't it better to win a spelling bee than to be able to draw the most gang symbols? Which is most likely to carry over into earning a living and surviving a full lifespan?

I hope we can re-teach society how to be ashamed of tearing down things and destroying the sense of safety that people should be able to take for granted in their own homes. I want to see new ways to build pride and a sense of caring, cooperative community. Most of all, I want Enos Park to be a place where people can be proud to live.

(May 1995)

~BUILDING COMMUNITY~

How Well Do You Know Your Neighbor?
Strong neighborhoods are built on strong connections between households. Please add up the points on the list below of all factors which apply to your four closest neighbors. These could be the people in the houses on either side of you and in front and back, other residents of your apartment building or people you know best on your block.

✦Neighbor? What neighbor?	0 points
✦Recognize neighbors and wave	1 point
✦Have talked with neighbor at least once	2 points
✦Know their first & last names (human & pet)	1 point each
✦Have been invited into their home as a guest	3 points
✦Routinely invite neighbors to parties & cookouts	5 points
✦Kids play together	5 points
✦Lend & borrow tools, recipes, assist each other	7 points
✦Attend Enos Park meetings together	10 points
✦Give each other keys to watch homes while gone	15 points
✦Marry the boy/girl next door	50 points

Totals:

Neighbor 1 ———

Neighbor 2 ———

Neighbor 3 ———

Neighbor 4 ———

Grand total ———

designed by Lola L. Lucas

25

Blueberries and Porch Swings

The next door neighbor started it—what choice did we have but to retaliate?

Becky had brought over rhubarb cake, hot from the oven, then two batches of home-made soup. Our honor was on the line so we fired a salvo over the fence of Blueberry Celebration Pie (two cups of heavy whipping cream, white chocolate and almonds, fresh, plump blue blueberries.) Ha! Take *THAT*!

Fortunately the neighborhood continues to be enchanted with Kevin's bagpipe playing instead of calling the police. It would definitely strain relations if they objected to him practicing "Scotland the Brave" when he gets home from work. I think he rather likes being besieged by children begging him to play. The little girls from the houses on both sides of us love to pretend to be highland dancing and, while they don't have prize-winning form, they seem to be getting a very aerobic workout. They scamper from one end of their porches to the other and whirl about in a gale of giggles. I like sitting on the swing, watching cars slow down to take in the sight of the Scottish rampant lion flag flying, a piper piping and four maids a-dancing. Some even stop to snap pictures.

It's idyllic, like small town Americana as the screen doors whoosh and the sun tea brews in the longer light of the evenings. Last weekend we trooped next door to play board games with friends from the bicycle club then on Sunday we cooked hot dogs and filled up the back deck with adults, children, dogs and cats as repayment for Bruce's help in assembling the grill. You know that little quiz I devised years ago that the *Banner* runs occasionally on how well do you know your neighbors? We're pushing 40 points now with the houses on either side and it makes for a lovely, safe feeling. When I hear voices in the driveway, I know who they are. I've been told the life history of the retired magician's rabbit, Magic, and of

Ruby the cat's unfortunate proclivity for chipmunks. Keys are traded, eggs borrowed, and tools loaned. As Jo said one day with evident satisfaction, "This is a real house, a family house. This is the way life is meant to be." Standing under a huge oak tree with light filtering down on well-tended gardens, I couldn't have agreed with her more.

What does it take to extend that sense of peace and of safety to every home in Springfield? If I had the answers for unemployment, educational reform, eliminating crime and rebuilding strong families, I'd give 'em, believe me, I wouldn't hold out on you. As it is, it looks like a long process to restore much of what we once took for granted. How can we pry people away from their televisions and get them to talk to one another again? (People do seem willing enough to jabber away on those radio call-in programs. Perhaps Marilyn could host one to show Rush how it should be done!)

This July, let's celebrate an independence from the tyranny of crime and decay. If we're going to fire on our neighbors, I *strongly* recommend blueberries instead of bullets.

(July 1995)

The Cheesecake Bake-off

Yes, we wanted the fourth annual invitational cheesecake bake-off to be a flaming success, but not that sort! I had a bad turn when I opened the Sunday paper and found that a building in Washington Park had burned the previous evening. Wait a minute! How am I going to contact all those people? Where am I going to *put* them? The bake-off has outgrown our dining room so I'd rented the pavilion for the afternoon because it seemed cheaper than buying a larger house. However, it was a structure by the tennis courts that burned, not the WPA lodge-style pavilion. Whew.

We had several phone calls that morning to verify that the event was still on. At noon we trundled laundry baskets filled with supplies over to the pavilion and had an hour to set up. The Murphy girls, bless them, arrived early and pitched in while their father, Joe, and Kevin quite literally manned the barricades. (Traffic had to be directed around the Hike and Bike barriers that go up on Sundays.) Before long, what had been a nondescript room had been decorated, coffee pots were merrily perking and Kevin's vegetable beef soup was simmering. Next, the guests and their cheesecakes began to arrive. We've almost forgotten exactly why we started four years ago but after the first event, the thing began to snowball. All told, we had 56 attendees ranging in age from one to 75, and a magnificent array of 15 varieties of cheesecakes set out on three tables.

Each entrant received a commemorative cake server with real stainless steel but faux crystal handles and we gave framed certificates to winners in each category. Cynthia Mehl of Enos Park won the Traditional Cheesecake title for a luscious New York style with a thin layer of lemon in the center. 10 year old Skylar Morris won Best Flavored for his Turtle Cheesecake which also received an ultimate accolade: the judges reported that after they'd sampled all 15 varieties, they went back for a full slice of Skylar's. My mother and my husband were in hot competition for Most

Unusual. Kevin's non-dairy tofu and fructose entry had fresh strawberries going for it, but Mom's new German Chocolate Cake/Cheesecake recipe edged ahead for the award. The Most Artistic Presentation went to my colleague, Marsha Jaeggi, for a brownie caramel cheesecake with a latticework topping that looked too good to eat. People nonetheless dove in and it was the only one with absolutely no leftovers. As the organizer, I retain the prerogative of giving an Almost Anything Award which went to Chuck Orwig, for a beautifully presented coconut extravaganza. ("What are you making?" I was asked a few times in the weeks leading up to the bake-off. I'd smile and reply, "The event.")

Although we had four diligent official judges, everyone got to vote for the most popular entry overall. A friend I've known for decades, Jim Buck, won the Grand Prize ribbon and a crystal trophy. No one was more surprised than he, since it was his first ever cheesecake, made with a recipe found on the Internet. Oh my, that Apple Praline was gray in color and didn't look like much, but it sat up and sang on the tongue!

Cherry cheesecakes, peppermint with delicious pink swirls, deep dish blueberry, white chocolate macadamia nut—not a clunker in the bunch, the level of competition keeps rising each year. And why do we do it? Why go to the trouble and the expense? Well, it's worth it for the delighted smiles of our friends and neighbors, the exclamations, the people hugging each other, toddlers running, teens wandering off to their own conversations. My sister-in-law said to my mother, "Kevin and Lola have more fun than anyone I know," and that's a reputation I'm willing to live with. We made a lot of people happy and in the process, we had a blast. The only downside is that I'll have to wait about another 364 days until we can do it all over again. Give us another few years, and I predict we'll be out at the fairgrounds.

"Creating community" is an abstract notion. Getting friends and neighbors together and feeding them is a joyous reality. My suggestion is to host your own chili cook-off or chocolate theme supper soon, just add people and stir.

(April 2002)

Virtual Communities

In our list of favorite things to do in Springfield, hanging out at Barnes & Noble swilling espresso and reading magazines would easily make the top five. There's nothing like a bit of latte foam on the lip and the delicious taste of new information, sweet as one of the pastries. Sometimes we buy the magazines, sometimes not, but I daresay B&N has made a tidy profit on our twin addictions to print and caffeine.

Recently I was there reading about what defines community in an age of increasingly complex communications. Is there truly such a thing as a neighborhood in cyberspace? That's a yes and no proposition. Cyberspace is really nothing other than digitally encoded bits of energy which now encircle the globe, linked by satellites and computer systems in the Internet. And what a bewildering place that is! It's as wild and wooly as the Old West, as frantic as the gold rush, as people venture out into the Net. There simply is nothing too bizarre or obscure to rate its own newsgroup of like-minded individuals.

For several years, Kevin and I have been connected to Prodigy and America on Line (AOL). In the early days of our marriage, we'd squabble over computer time though we've gotten more considerate of each other as our initial infatuation with the service waned. We each live in cyberspace communities with friends who've become real people to us. We exchange Christmas cards with these folks, talk to them on the phone, and sometimes have even met them in real life. (In the bad old days, wives sometimes had to haul their husbands out of the corner taverns; I just peek into Kevin's study and see him at the computer, hanging out in a virtual bar in cyberspace with his cronies from the submarine board.) Although we share interests with these people, is it a real community?

In cyberspace, no one is judged by appearances: age, gender, race and all those other factors we automatically tabulate at a glance become moot points. One is valued by how well one writes and by the qualities of personality that can come across in print. Still, all it takes is hitting the Delete key to eliminate e-mail and thus communication. It's not that simple in a neighborhood of bricks and aluminum siding. Actual communities don't have what's known as a "bozo filter" to block out objectionable people—more's the pity, sometimes. Yet there is a level of commitment, of shared burdens, that continues to bind people together in the real world. It's a pleasure to have friends all over the country but it's not the same as the fun of having people over for Sunday brunch to see their smiles, hug them, and feed them waffles.

Physical communities take a lot of maintenance work while cyber communities are like an ocean, washing together and apart because when it's no longer fun in cyberspace, people just wander off to something else. The Net offers unparalleled opportunities to collect new information from other groups interested in neighborhood preservation but it'll never replace the face to face caring of the real people who live next door. Perhaps a time will come when virtual reality allows us to "see" whatever we want to in our dwellings but, at present, it takes work to make those images reality.

(April 1995)

Friendships (FIPLAWIT)

FIPLAWIT was one of my best ideas ever.

It's said that imitation is the sincerest form of flattery, but what about enthusiastically studying what others like? FIPLAWIT is my acronym for "Find Interesting People and Learn About What Interests Them." I'm not a people person—no, as a dyed in the wool introvert I can actually be quite shy. Performing is one thing, but having to make small talk, that's draining. I got over being standoffish with an amazing realization: people are just books on the hoof! When I understood that, it made conversation much easier. I began thinking in terms of what I could learn from others.

Given limitless funds I might have enjoyed being a perpetual student, a so-called "slackademic." Since there's dog food to put in the bowl, I have to 9 to 5 it like the rest of the world. Then one day it dawned on me that if I taught college, I could stay there and they'd pay me for it! What a scam! So I teach a few classes each year, mostly for the fun of it. Although I keep up with trends in my field that way, I still have a lot of energy and curiosity left over.

See, I already know what I know. On dull days I remember a line from a Bruce Springsteen song, "I'm just sittin' 'round here, tired and bored with myself." To find out what someone else knows, ah, now there's some sport to that. My first FIPLAWIT was when I was a sophomore in high school with a crush on a senior who seemed very mature and sophisticated to me. I tagged along on his interests and learned about electronic music and kinetic light sculptures. I may not listen to John Cage anymore, but I have fond memories of the things people will do to a piano in the name of art. I maintained my passion for light sculptures, though, because what is a kaleidoscope but whirling patterns of color?

The best FIPLAWIT experiences combine intellectual admiration with personal affection. For example, my aunt-by-choice Jackie Jackson—resident legend in Enos Park—was a founding faculty member at Sangamon State, now the University of Illinois at Springfield. She teaches in a full tilt take-no-prisoners style that I try to emulate. Because of Jackie I've read books I wouldn't have considered on my own and I've seen some deeply weird films. Like her, I enjoy early Ursula LeGuin, but I'm just not ever going to be wild about Lewis Carroll. Well, I tried it and now I have an informed opinion instead of an unformed one. It's said that real education replaces an empty mind with an open one.

My friend Jim McKee was the first person I ever asked how it felt to be a FIPLAWIT project. "It's just what you do, isn't it?" He seemed rather surprised at the question. Well, yes. From him I acquired exposure to fly fishing and by extension, the books of David James Duncan. I also got Shane MacGowan's Irish punk rock and a renewed interest in theater, dance, literature, poetry and politics. Even New Jersey got tossed into the deal. (Their new state motto should be "It's nice—really!")

French author Anais Nin wrote, "Each friend represents a world in us, a world possibly not born until they arrive, and it is only by this meeting that a new world is born." We find ourselves reflected in others and we can acquire new thoughts, traits, or ways of being from them. Friendship is a wonderful way to cross-pollinate ideas, or as I like to say, "We are the sum total of the people we have loved."

We have such a wealth of human capital in Enos Park! People who are smart enough to invest in a good thing, committed enough to hold to their course, home owners with energy, creativity and enthusiasm. Who knows what worlds of wonder are inside the minds and hearts of your neighbors? Try talking to them to discover just how interesting they really are and you'll find yourself enriched.

(September 2003)

Better than Free

"Better than free" is the slogan that a bank printed on my checks, touting no charges for accounts. But whenever I see it, I think of something completely different.

Finnegan knows the meaning of "better than free." He's the easiest dog to collar that I've ever met. He lifts his head, brown eyes shining with adoration, to have his house collar or his outdoor gear put on. To him, it serves much the same function as our wedding rings. It means, "I belong to someone, I have a home!" Who knows how long he ran as a stray? When we got him, he was filthy, matted, wormy and starved. He understood the line from the old Janis Joplin song about "freedom's just another word for nothing left to lose." Was he happy to give up being The Wild Poodle of Rochester to become the low dog on the totem pole with his new sister Fiona biting his neck? Yes, he was. He traded freedom to wander for rules, schedules, commands—and also two people who welcome him to lie between them as he shivers when the thunderstorms roll over the prairie.

As for me, each Independence Day marks another anniversary in Springfield since 1991. Go ahead and laugh: I had planned to live here for a year or so and then move back to St. Louis. At first, it felt claustrophobic, like living under a bell jar. It was impossible then to drive 15 minutes in any direction without being in a corn field. (Now, of course, it's 20 minutes.) It was both painful and liberating to pack the last of my belongings into the car and head north on I-55 for a new life. I knew my mother was sad, even though it was only a two-hour drive because it meant I'd become a visitor instead of a casual drop-in at my parents' house. I was trading the security of my home town for a new life with Kevin, stepping into a different set of obligations.

There are also bonds that tie us to friends and neighbors. Becky next door had probably—and reasonably—given up hope that we'd ever get our yard in order. Part of it is sheer ignorance about plants but also there are competing priorities since Kevin and I both work full time and teach part-time. She was bemoaning that she'd gotten her yard done and had nothing much left to do for the rest of her summer vacation. Wanna do ours? She tucked right into it with a passion that suggested a lot of pent-up frustration as she'd watched our roses go wild and our bushes grow over the walkway. We've responded so far with a bottle of good wine and a tin of Scottish shortbread but I doubt that will be the end of it. We are obligated and I don't mind being in her debt. Other times, I've shared career and scholarship information with her teen-aged daughter and hired her son to deliver bookcases. We have her mother join us for supper when she's in town. We all cooperate with the shared driveway.

Recently we looked at a house that sits on three acres. It was wonderfully private but also seemed lonely. Maybe I've just gotten used to living at close quarters where we smell cooking, hear garage doors going up and down and listen to kids practice their music lessons. When there's a voice near my window, I know whose it is. Talking between porches is easy as we sit out and wave at neighbors walking toward the park. We can quickly get a group together to go see a movie, come over for board games or for impromptu parties. I've yet to use my crystal and china but there have been paper plates a-plenty over the years.

To my mind, it's important to allow other people to do things for you, and for you to be ready to help them. Reciprocity is more than a mechanical trade-off; it's a full and willing heart that looks for ways to be of service. It's taking one's place in the great dance of life, whether it's as dramatic as sandbagging against a flood or as simple as keeping an ear open to monitor children playing on the sidewalks. It's the bonds of living together in a community that make a collection of households a neighborhood in Enos Park. And to me, that's much better than free.

(July 2000)

~DÉCOR AND ARCHITECTURE~

Illinois State Museum

I have fond memories of the Illinois State Museum because Kevin took me there to a murder mystery evening on our fourth date. It was the first time I'd ever been to Springfield other than just driving through to Chicago. Recently I was showing the museum to a friend who was here for a visit and discovered a new permanent exhibition called "At Home in the Heartland." It traces domestic life from the French and Indian days to a modern teenager's closet. It's an interactive exhibit in which you examine choices, make your selection between the alternatives and then find out what the person really did. It can be as simple as deciding whether to build a table, have one made or buy it from an estate sale—or as vivid as the woman from Springfield who had to decide whether to go with her husband to California, have him go first and send for her later or refuse to go at all. "Don't go! Don't go!!" we want to yell at her across the years but she went with the Donner party to that snowy mountain pass.

Then as now, what we buy to furnish our homes is based on several factors. Cost is a major one, but that's closely followed by availability, social mores, current styles and personal preferences. (The exhibit told of a circuit riding preacher who threatened not to return to visit a family until the miserly father bought some decent furniture plus fabric to make new dresses for his womenfolk.) Nowadays if we decide to save money by making something instead of buying it, it's seldom more complicated than curtains, but back then people crafted elaborate furniture and household items. Winter was a time for carving wood and tatting lace since there was no television or Nintendo to distract them from the howling winds of the prairie.

The Sears Roebuck and the Montgomery Ward catalogs ushered in a whole new world of machine-made, cheap and available products and the clutter ratio in the full size sample rooms rises sharply. One exhibit poses the question of where to put the new-fangled telephone contraption. You make your choice—perhaps sensibly near the bathtub—then see that the family actually installed it in the downstairs hallway. Moving forward in time, the recreated 1950's rec room begins to draw cries of "I had one of those!" Remember? Knotty pine paneling, a hi-fi, those black ceramic panthers? Personally, I could relate to the room with the lava lamp and the Danish modern stereo stocked with Beatles albums. One display showed what a polyester-clad couple from 1977 requested for wedding presents (a year's supply of toilet paper, newspaper subscriptions, a vacuum cleaner) and what they actually got: silver chafing dishes and yes, a fondue pot, although oddly enough, in blue instead of harvest gold or avocado.

Obviously, we still face the same sort of choices now as we decide what to spend our time and money on for our living spaces. How do we create something cozy enough to come back to after a hard day of slaving over a hot computer? We make trade-offs all the time. For example, we're tempted to buy a marble-topped coffee table at the mall but the roof needs repair and we want to get a new hot water heater. One would add to our sense of prestige when company comes over but the other two protect our investment in our home and will ultimately save us money. Decisions, decisions. Good sense will win out, but not without a struggle.

Our Enos Park House Tours are a wonderful way to see how our neighbors have made their choices. (Maybe we can even organize ourselves for a neighborhood-wide yard sale day to re-shuffle and recycle possessions around.) Enjoying our homes, inside and out, gives us the sense of pride to keep pushing to make this a better and better place to live.

(April 1993)

Resources for Rehabbers

Has *This Old House* ever turned instead into your own personal *Money Pit*? Do you long for Bob and Norm (or at least Tim and Al) to come and do some *Home Improvements*? Doing it yourself takes more than blood, sweat and tears—it takes information and resources.

Some excellent publications offer ideas on restoring your home to its former grandeur, or in some more modest dreams, to simple inhabitability. (The fall house tour showed some examples of genuine urban pioneering with one couple living in two rooms while working on the remaining 12.) There are specialty catalogs such as *Renovator's Supply* that offer reproductions of plumbing and lighting fixtures as well as wallpaper designed to cover aging plaster. *The Old House Journal* has both a monthly magazine of practical tips and an annual compendium of resources for the rehabber. Their book catalog includes lush views of opulent Victorian interiors. There are listings of commercial/professional restoration services and products in each issue. Best of all is the back page with the "remuddling" atrocity of the month.

Victorian Homes expands the scope from houses to cultural artifacts and customs of the era. You're more likely to find hints here for a proper croquet game than for stripping woodwork with a heat gun. A similarly titled magazine, *Victoria*, is primarily about fashions and accessories that promise a more genteel, lavender-scented existence far, far from the expressway of modern life.

The National Trust for Historic Preservation has a monthly magazine, *Preservation*. Although the focus has generally been on public and commercial restorations, they occasionally run issues on work being done on individual homes. Their strong suit is discussing community activism and government regulations which have an impact on rehabbing. These are the folks who have degrees in historic sites management, preservation technology and who go wild talking about the decline of UDAGs (Urban Development Action Grants, such as the ones that underwrote the renaissance of St. Louis' Union Station.)

Lincoln Library's Sangamon Valley Collection has resources for researching your home's history. There may well be old photos with hints for how to recreate a side porch or return a roof line to its original shape. The library also has numerous books on caring for and repairing the older home. They're needed, because with vintage homes we get lots and lots of character and charm along with old pipes and sometimes demented wiring. To live in them takes more patience, perseverance, pluck and old-fashioned fortitude than to just tear them down and move to brand new subdivisions. We recycle the buildings and build a link between the past and future.

(November 1992)

Renovating Old Houses

The stories are often quite similar but to me, they never grow monotonous. The plot usually involves a heroine living a seemingly full life while secretly feeling haunted by a sense of incompleteness. Then one day, there's an unforeseen turning. Suddenly she finds her true love, newly met yet hauntingly familiar, as though her whole existence has been moving toward this moment. There's a sense of déjà vu, of coming home. Invariably, there are difficulties with legal issues, family members, and friends who urge her to abandon her beloved. Sometimes horrible, hideous secrets are revealed—some may even be deadly. On occasion, there's a ghost or two lurking from the past. Yet through her passion and perseverance, her pluckiness in the face of all odds, she's united with her adored in eternal, happily-ever-after commitment.

Romance novels? No, home decorating magazines.

My favorite articles are about women (or men or couples) who come upon an abandoned house and fall in love with it. Despite the lack of a For Sale sign, they track down the local lore and discover that the house has been sitting empty for years, even decades. They manage to purchase it and naturally, that's only the start. It turns out that the lovely old vicarage is a deathtrap with wiring and plumbing in some crazed confusion. When walls are removed, rot and worse is revealed. The sewer turns out to be a nasty joke played by the local public works department. Nonetheless, they eventually have black and white before pictures to proudly tuck into the corner of the full-color extravaganza on their remodeled gem.

I particularly liked an article about a former hunting lodge where one obstacle was removing hoof marks from the plank floors because during Prohibition, inebriated riders had a bad habit of spurring their mounts through the house.

You can find this type of story in *House Beautiful* or *Old House Interiors* or any of several magazines, but I love best the British periodicals, such as *Period Homes*, *Period Living* and *25 Beautiful Homes*. The Brits don't have to settle for houses a century or three old, tops: they can get into renovating decrepit structures five or even nine hundred years of age, half-timbered thatched cottages made of wattle. It boggles my mind that in a rainy climate, houses made of twigs daubed with mud could last so long with no special intervention. In comparison, some people think it's impossible to keep brick houses up in Springfield after a measly century—"too old, too far gone, unsafe at such an advanced age. Can't be done."

I read such articles avidly, with hopes of picking up good advice. One example was of a couple who offered a ridiculously low sum for a small castle in Wales. The owner took them up on it immediately and went capering off down the cobblestones to freedom. Really, that should have been their first clue. By the time they were ready to invite decorating magazine photographers in, they had undoubtedly rediscovered many time over what Churchill meant about blood, sweat and tears.

I have my own lingering fantasy about finding a stone house in the woods with diamond paned windows and an overgrown garden. There's an arched wooden door with wide iron hinges. Kevin and I buy it and set out to restore it. Before long (hey, it's my fantasy!) the floors gleam, the kitchen and bathrooms have been remodeled, our oriental rugs, tapestries and velvet furniture are all in place, and our housekeeper meets us at the door, with fires blazing cheerfully in the grates and supper ready. It's like a scene from one of those Thomas Kinkade calendars, all warm and sublimely cozy.

There's always the trade-off between reality and hopes, but I remind myself that what seems dream-like can be quite real. I'll either have to keep looking for my ideal home or build it. But I can't give it up. True love is like that.

May your home be your castle, too!

(November 1998)

Remuddling

Oh, if only our neighbors *knew*! We go out for walks early in the morning when it's still cool and we scrutinize the houses for blocks around us. We actually notice when people put up a new wreath or have planted a different type of flowers. We track progress: hmmm, nice job of scraping, we murmur to each other, then we check what color the residents have decided to use for trim. One nondescript white house was transformed into a miniature painted lady with blue-grey paint and crimson decorations. Yard signs from construction companies and real estate agents are discussed. We rejoice as houses are rehabilitated and sigh and shake our heads over ones in decline.

Every now and then we've been tempted to turn in one to the *Old House Journal* feature called "Remuddling." It's a popular item on the last page of each issue showing updates which have gone horribly, horribly wrong. For example, some people do turretectomies, then slap siding over beautiful fish scale shingles for a "fresh new look." That sort also likes to paint varnished woodwork. Others replace graceful columns with cheap metal supports, rip off porches or put in gawky storm windows that ruin the proportions of the house. Remuddlers, given half a chance, would drill holes in the Sistine Chapel to hang a suspended ceiling of acoustic tile. (In our lovely blue house on 4th Street, someone had hammered nails into antique tiles on the fireplace hearth to put in wall to wall shag carpeting. The word "horsewhip" springs to mind.)

In the worst cases, one has to ask, "Why??" The mind boggles that someone could have conceived of something so ghastly and then carried it out. A good example of that is silver Mylar wallpaper with red velvet flocking. If you're a Baby Boomer or older, you may have actually seen some of this. Why would anyone design it? Who would initial the approval for it and send it to the shop floor to be manufactured in bolts? What store would carry it or customer buy and—heaven forbid—hang the stuff? Similarly, some remuddling is absolutely breath-taking in its audacity. *Why* would someone do that to an innocent house that never even had a chance to shriek and run away?

Fortunately, we haven't seen many that were that far gone. Often what we note are places where people have tried to cut corners to save money. Maybe they just plain didn't have it to spend, maybe it was investment property and they didn't want to diminish the cash flow. Maybe, in some cases, they honestly thought they were improving the house and making it more modern. An example is a grand old house which has been split up into several apartments. Well, that's hardly news in Springfield, but in this case, the stairway was put in the front of the building, then disguised with an ugly vertical-slatted construct painted pinkish-brown. It's not a pretty sight and it stands as a mute testimonial to the idea of down-zoning multi-families back to their original single family use whenever possible.

Kevin's become quite adept at spotting architectural styles and enjoys saying things like, "Ah, an Italianate with post-Federalist features" with dashing aplomb. It's the same sort of skill he uses to identify planes going overhead at a glance or even by the sound of their motors. At some point he decided that a good Queen Anne was every bit as interesting as a 1967 Boss Mustang.

Sometimes people make needed improvements because they're worried about what the neighbors will think. Well, we're them! We *are* looking and thinking and applauding! It's a source of great delight to us to see your houses well tended and lovingly restored. Thank you for making *your* home a vital part of the Enos Park neighborhood.

(September 1995)

Paint Brush Award

The nomination for May is 1108 North Third Street, the home of Reneé Frederick and Roy Pillischafske. The home has recently acquired a new coat of paint. Each month a home is nominated for the Paint Brush Award. Then in January the Board chooses the house among monthly nominees for the Golden Paint Brush Award. Nominations are always welcome.

Bathroom Remodeling

When recently looking at Dover Books reproductions of home plans from the 1920's, I was struck by the sheer lack of bathrooms because generally there was one per house on the second floor. I came across a couple where a toilet was provided near a back porch, or in a basement, but they had no sinks, which offends our modern sense of hygiene. Personal experience with living in old houses and looking at them on the market has shown that a makeshift basement shower was often present, if not specified in the plans. You may have one in your home: a rusty looking pipe by the water taps, perhaps even with one of those circular shower curtain holders. While you're down there, check for a horseshoe since many houses of that era had them for luck. (Note to file: people in other parts of the country do not think of cheese or salivate at the thought of horseshoes.)

I chanced on a magazine of house plans from the 1970's where the master bedrooms were supplied with their very own toilets, small sinks and showers. This provided a new height of luxury for parents suddenly freed from competing with their offspring for bathroom time. And in the bigger houses, which is to say those of about 2,000 square feet, there was usually a powder room on the first floor and maybe another ¾ bath in the basement near the rumpus room.

HGTV's *Dream House* follows people through all the phases of constructing a home, from design through housewarming party—or, in one memorable case, through litigation. One showed a house in Minnesota with an 800 square foot *closet*. Nowadays it's not uncommon to see bathrooms in homes that are only slightly smaller than some countries that issue stamps. I'm torn between desire for an extravagant bath and being appalled at wretched excess. In point of fact, I would like a whirlpool and a separate shower and a double sink and toilet in its own little room. OK, a walk-out garden patio, an exercise spa and a fireplace would be nice, too.

I have a theory that people in my age group who are building these palaces of privacy remember when the bathroom was the only place in the house with a lock on it. Ours was hotly contested, even with only four of us in the family. Perhaps the people who have them constructed are honoring a childhood vow: "One day I'll have my very own and nobody's gonna yell at me no matter how long I stay in there!" I've seen articles claiming that with a bathroom per bedroom, children are not developing character the way we did in the good old days when times were bad. However, I firmly believe that the opportunity to linger in a froth of bubbles beats a quick rub-a-dub with siblings pounding on the door.

We recently redid our own bathroom. Being a veteran of a previous bath and a kitchen remodel, I was prepared for it taking longer than scheduled and costing more than budgeted. All said and done, it went quite smoothly, thanks to good communication and respect on both sides. Before, Kevin would step into the bathtub if I came in to brush my teeth, but now we can easily fit four people in at a time. (They come in to admire it, you understand.) The turning point was when it dawned on me to move the wall between the bath and the sitting room. Everything else fell into place after that and we now have a bath almost as nice as the one we had at Fourth Street.

If you've got a claw foot tub, a pedestal sink and vintage hardware, do NOT throw them out. There's a thriving trade in selling them and the reproductions have outrageous price tags. In Enos Park, you may well have the type of bath that others are trying to copy in decorating magazines. Whether it's Gucci handbags or genuine Victorian cottages, there's something to be said for the smug feeling of, "I've got the original!"

(April 1999)

Quest for Bargains

They loaded some of it into their car, drove away and I danced on the porch, happy, happy, happy! I'd finally sold the bathtub, marble top and cabinets!

It had seemed like such a good idea at the time when I bought that bathroom display from Lowe's. They were the cherry cabinets of my dreams and in the adrenaline surging euphoria, I forgot that the space for our upstairs tub was 54" instead of the standard 60". Or perhaps I thought that we'd find a way to shoehorn it in, knock out some walls, maybe rotate it, put it where the sink was—let's just say that hope overcame measurements and good sense. I spent months playing with scale model paper versions of the cabinets and fixtures until finally it all became clear: move the south non-load bearing wall by two feet and admit that the tub and dressing table weren't going to fit unless I (shudder) had plumbing connections moved. That hurt. I'd been particularly in love with the cherry paneled apron on the tub because it looked so classy, like the self-covered buttons my mother always favored.

Anyone who's done remodeling knows that you get to pick two out of three: fast, cheap, or good. I regret that I sometimes fall prey to what I call the Baltic Syndrome. Ever play Monopoly? I always liked buying the first two purple properties, Mediterranean and Baltic. Sure the rents were low but so was the purchase price and it was relatively easy to build hotels compared to the old money green places, Park Place and Boardwalk. The downside of that approach in real life is that I sometimes drag home great bargains, then take years to figure out how to use them.

Trying to do things on the cheap has meant buying things such as a double wall oven in a cabinet that teetered alarmingly. I had a pair of French doors that waited for years in the garage until inspiration struck and I realized I could build a closet and use them. (Those of you with older homes probably know all about the dearth of closets in them. The truth is, they simply didn't own as much stuff a century ago as we do now.)

Odds are that our bathroom got done sooner than it might have because Kevin balked at having a bathtub in the front parlor for more than half a year. He was also getting testy about the left-over cabinets being on the front porch. An ad in *The Shopper* turned out to be a great way to meet lots of nice people who came to look at the items. Many convinced themselves, regardless of what I'd told them repeatedly on the phone, that the dressing table could be turned into a sink. I admit it, I had wild plans like that when I got it, too, and then ended up buying a vanity base and doing it right. (Good and fast, but not cheap.)

At long last there was a call from someone who'd seen the ad. Did I still have the tub and cabinets? Oh yes. She arrived with plans for a bathroom extension for her first floor and the cherry would match her kitchen cabinets. As a veteran garage sale fanatic, she was confident that nicks in the tub could be fixed and a bit of Olde English scratch cover polish would do wonders for the cabinet. She wasn't quite sure when they'd actually use all the pieces, mind you, but they could go into their garage in the meantime. Seldom have I had the pleasure of meeting such a kindred soul. I could've wept when we agreed to a price that was 25 cents on the dollar of the retail price but still meant I was recovering 2/3 of what I'd spent in my overly optimistic frenzy when I said, "Why not? I'll take them all!" at Lowe's.

As the flowers open and the trees leaf out in Enos Park, remember that hope springs most eternal in a remodeler's heart.

(May 2001)

~HOLIDAYS~

Reflections in a Silver Ball

Last year was our first Christmas in Enos Park. For our annual open house, we asked that all our friends and relatives bring us an ornament which had hung on their own trees to start ours in our new home, our new marriage. And ornaments they brought! Mirrored bells from Mexico, tiny sleighs, expensive crystal—and one that was a silver ball with a yellow stripe, rusted in spots. The top of that one is corroded; you remember those metal caps which held the wire that had to be carefully fit over the branch then put into the glass part of the ornament? It's more than 40 years old. Nowadays there are books on the value of antique and collectible ornaments but without looking at it, I can tell you this one is priceless. My parents hung it on their tree, including their last Christmas together a few months before I was born. (My father died when I was three months old.) Each Christmas, the number of ornaments from that period dwindled. Unlike the plastic ones that bounce, these were fragile glass and there were casualties each season during the unpacking, hanging and removing them from the tree.

So this particular ornament is very special. It says something to me about love and continuity and the importance of honoring and preserving the past while using it to make an even better future. Our neighborhood's homes are like that, too. They require careful treatment to make sure they keep on being beautiful and that they are there for future generations to cherish as we pass them down. What are any of us, really, except caretakers for what we've been given so briefly?

Some neighborhoods have shattered when they dropped from the mainstream and declined. Some just get shabbier and shabbier. But the lucky ones, like Enos Park, don't shatter, they bounce back. People get involved, they clean it up, fix it up. They get mad about trash or crime, *and they do something about it because the neighborhood is worth it.* We stand up and say "This is our HOME" and kick the drug dealers off the streets. Less dramatically but just as importantly over the long run, we scrape the paint and plant the flowers. We watch our neighbors' houses for them, we keep an eye on their children as they play because they are *all* ours. We sit on porches and wave to the folks going by. And that's what makes Enos Park a very, very wonderful place to call home.

Whether you and yours are celebrating Christmas, Hanukkah, Kwanza, the Winter Solstice or other holiday, may you find as much joy in your heart as I've seen reflected in that silver ball.

(December 1992)

Holiday Shopping

They're off and running! Well, OK, they're off the starting line with a tummy full of turkey, waddling into the holiday shopping season. Some started early, at 4 a.m. when Wal-Mart's doors opened on the Friday after Thanksgiving. The newspaper reported that 80 people were lined up before dawn. Parking lots are packed and consumers are shopping but are they *buying*, fret the retailers and the economists. For the shoppers, it's good news as nervous shopkeepers run sale after sale to tempt us.

There are those who have all their presents purchased and wrapped by October (with paper they undoubtedly bought at New Year's sales) but I'm not one of them. So far, I'm barely inching off the starting line for the holidays and the thought of putting up a tree, decorating the house and all the rest seems daunting. But I have a secret ally. Where folks used to turn to Bing Crosby or Frosty the Snowman, I have Weird Al and the other artists on the inspired CD, *Twisted Christmas*. Soon we'll get it out and begin laughing at the idea of Santa stuck in the chimney or the McKenzie Brothers' quest for a beer instead of a partridge in a pear tree. Friends tell us the CD of barking dogs and cats yowling carols is a hoot, too. Are we irreverent? No, we just enjoy being able to sing something as silly as "Percy, the Lonely Poinsettia" as we drive the highways, shuttling between our families' homes. Heavens, we don't want anyone's grandma to be *really* run over by a reindeer!

We also play New Age and Celtic carols and I dearly love to listen to Mario Lanza sing as I bake cookies. His voice brings back decades of memories. Each family has its own traditions and they can accumulate over the years as surely as hangers multiply in closets. Kevin and I have more and more decorations and we enjoy our annual ritual of getting a new ornament together each year. It doesn't have to have the date inscribed, it's sufficient that we can remember where we got it as we put it up in years to come.

Soon we'll be taking cookies, loaves of bread and/or doggie biscuits to our neighbors up and down the block. It costs so little but the reward of their smiles or wagging tails when they see a plate of goodies is priceless. With any luck, the local children will put on a pageant to rival the production they did this fall. They had printed programs, popcorn, costumes, the whole works. (But the six-year-old Prince Charming was only willing to shake hands with Cinderella at the end of the play, he wasn't about to kiss a *girl*.)

The question is, if we could wrap up something and give it to Enos Park, what would it be? How large would the box have to be? Could we get a ribbon around it? A good plan for the area would fit tidily in a shirt box with room left over. A major grant for homeowner renovation could be slipped into an envelope. It might take a bigger container, though, if we gave ourselves enough paint to do every house that needs it. I have a wonderful image of Santa standing in the back of an 18-wheeler, handing out rakes and tools with ribbons around them!

The best gift we can give each other in Enos Park is our pledge to work together to make this an area where families and businesses and dreams can grow. Blessings to you and yours for the holidays!

(December 1995)

Life Goes On

This year, I find myself stroking velvet tree skirts and fingering gold braid and fringe on elaborate stockings. I'm entranced by the glitter of baubles hung from displays, and even amused by an artificial tree with fiber optics in its pseudo-pine needles. The hand towels decorated with snowflakes and Santas seem droll, like a little joke to share with guests. Sleigh ride images on doormats welcome friends into the house. I've even had to fight down an impulse to buy holiday china with matching glasses and utensils and serving pieces and linens—the list goes on and on, even unto the red and green storage bins to pack it away at the end of the season. It's all magical and enchanting again.

Last Christmas was very different. It was a cruel hoax, a commercial horror of ugly products jostling on the shelves. The carols were discordant, whether played by Muzak or sung by neighbors on our doorstep. I did 90% of my shopping one afternoon in one store, glad to be done with it, disgusted that it had to be done at all. We didn't put up a tree, so the ornaments stayed in the basement. It was a Christmas of trying to go on, to stay normal in a profoundly changed world.

Mamaw passed away last October and I really don't remember much about Thanksgiving '97. The grief was even too fresh to make our traditional jokes about her and turkeys. (Three decades before, we'd been packing leftovers for my grandfather's lunchbox; he worked the evening shift as a night watchman. "Does Pampaw want a turkey sandwich?" I asked. "No, don't fix him one, I don't like turkey," said Mamaw and we teased her about that forever after.) I wrote her eulogy and much of it revolved around food, from the fruits and vegetables she grew to her cooking and canning and to her passion for going out to restaurants. For Mamaw, food was love made visible. Her kitchen produced an endless stream of dumplings, greens and cobblers from a pinch of this, a handful of that. She learned to cook on a wood stove in an Arkansas cabin while flappers danced in speakeasies and soldiers fought the war to end all wars in Europe. In her lifetime, she went from breaking her arm on a hand-crank of a Model T Ford to watching humans walk on the moon on her color television. She was nearly 87 so I used to tease her, "Ival Mae, if only the good die young, you done ruined your reputation!" and she'd laugh hugely.

Life goes on. Time fuzzes the edges of memory so that loss isn't a jagged gash. It transmutes pain into warm memories, stories told around the dinner table that bring laughter again. Gradually, those who've gone before settle into their new roles as invisible participants. We don't set a place for them but they're present, still part of the family.

"Joy is the shadow cast by pain," read my fortune cookie this week and indeed the holidays are bittersweet as years both take away and give. This past summer I've gone to the wedding of my cousin who used to ride horsy-back on me on Mamaw's living room floor. Love and loss string together like Christmas lights, strand after strand of memory winding around. That glow keeps us warm and connected as families.

May you and yours find much love and joy during in holidays.

(December 1998)

CMS Motor Pool

At its best, the holiday season adds a sparkle to the eyes as bright as a snowflake caught dancing in a streetlight's beam, along with smiles from strangers warm as hot chocolate after a sleigh ride. It's magical as we burn candles, fireplaces and strands of bulbs to triumph over the darkness that thuds on us by 5 p.m. "Wouldn't it be wonderful," my mother often says, "if it could just be like this always."

I've found something close, something almost as good as Santa and elves all year 'round at a seemingly unlikely place: Central Management Services' motor pool. I work for the state and travel all over Illinois from Galena to Carbondale with Chicago as my second home. During the fall training season—mercifully just wrapped up—I have to re-introduce myself to my coworkers when I come back in from the road. The people I see most often become Mel, Jerry and Gary as I pick up state cars at the garage on First Street. By 7 a.m. Mel's already been there for a while when Kevin drops me off. "Where to this time?" he asks cheerfully, and then enters my destination into his computer. Jerry gets the keys and soon has a car warming up, windows scraped of ice. I think that they like me in particular and give me extra special service: I have a sneaking suspicion that everyone else feels the same way when they check out a car.

Past a certain point I feel silly sending in comment sheets to their supervisor. What more can be said about consistent perfection? It's redundant to keep writing that the car was in great shape mechanically, it was scrupulously clean, that the staff was exceptional in courtesy, promptness and friendliness. Over time I've learned about the guys' families, pets, hobbies and dreams so each trip is a chance to catch up on what's new. I remember when Gary got contact lenses and announced he'd taken up dancing but nowadays we mostly talk about our dogs. I never cease to be amazed at the level of caring service they give because it makes me feel more safe, more secure when I'm out traveling alone to someplace that's only a dot on the map when I set out.

Granted, I do my part to make it a successful relationship. I pick up the cars and return them on schedule, even if it means pulling in late at night after 14 hours on the road. I've always brought them back undamaged and without tickets. (But I still shudder remembering one left turn I made in Chicago at the wrong place and how the on-coming driver's reflexes were all that kept my record spotless.) If they don't have a Taurus, I'll cheerfully drive anything they give me because I have utter faith in how they've kept it up, whether the car has seven miles on it or over 100,000. I depend on them—I literally trust them with my life each time I get behind the wheel.

I'd like to do a study comparing my guys with a state motor pool someplace else that's dysfunctional, where the workers are surly and slovenly and couldn't care less if their cars break down or their bald tires go flat. I would be willing to bet a year's salary that the CMS motor pool is more cost efficient because drivers feel comfortable reporting cars' small glitches before they turn into big mechanical problems. Intangibles such as the staff's cheerful smiles end up as plump black numbers on the bottom line. These guys are the anti-Dilberts, running an operation mixed with equal parts of common sense, competence and courtesy. If I ever write a best-selling management book, it'll be *Everything I Needed to Know about Customer Service I Learned at the CMS Motor Pool*.

Each holiday season I take them cookies or a tin of popcorn as a small way to thank them for taking such good care of me. I'll also give them copies of this issue of *The Banner* wrapped in a big red bow. Just as surely as there are vicious cycles, there are benevolent circles where kindness flows and is redoubled as it goes 'round and 'round between people who like and trust each other. What we call "Christmas spirit" doesn't have to be confined to the month of December. It's a state of mind that can last right through shamrocks, fireworks and jack o'lanterns with "peace on earth, goodwill toward all" each day in Enos Park, in Springfield, and in the world.

(December 1997)

Rezelations

"I'm making my New Year's rezelations," said my friend Ellison at lunch and then she laughed because she'd mingled several words together into a new concept. In trying to say "resolution" and "revelation" and "realization" at the same time, she'd hit upon the type of vow that we all want to be able to make as the calendar starts fresh. A rezelation is not a half-hearted promise of better behavior—it's a veritable light on the road to Damascus: total, unequivocal, impossible to go back on. It's not just knowing that a change is needed—it's revealing the truth at a deep level and acting upon it.

It's said that a good doctor is one who can tell you what's wrong with you if you don't smoke and you're not overweight. Those two items figure into many resolutions—whole industries are built around smoking cessation and weight reduction. I'm sure that world-weary cashiers see Nicorette and Lean Cuisine packages cross their scanners for two weeks in January, followed by Camels and Hagen Daz the rest of the year. Hope springs eternal and it keeps hypnotists in business as they travel a circuit offering to mesmerize hotel ballrooms full of people, drawn by promises of an easy, painless way to get rid of their problems. They're looking for a shortcut to a rezelation, a one-way ticket to a new life.

I've had a couple of rezelations where all the world stopped and poised perfectly in a moment of decision. The most striking was on Feb. 15, 1992, driving along I-55 when I told Kevin I wasn't going to drink alcohol anymore. There was a clarity to that, a sense of power and redemption within that instant that saw me through a radical change in habits. I'd been drinking far too much and for the wrong reasons, self-medicating instead of dealing with some very real issues. But I had several good role models for going cold turkey. My grandfather used to tell of a night when he was driving a horse-drawn wagon through a storm and how he'd vowed to stop drinking if he could just get across a bridge and home safely to his family. His wild days were abruptly over. Tom, an outplacement client of mine, told me how he'd been sitting on the hood of his car one evening, getting drunk as usual, until he looked at the beer can in his hand, weighed it against his family and put it down, never to pick up another.

I've had help in the past seven years from what I call "temperance dreams." In them, I've taken a sip from a glass and discovered that it was wine or a mixed drink. When I wake up, I'm horrified to have broken my years of not touching the stuff even in cough syrup—then grateful and relieved to find it was only a dream. It's enough to keep me on the straight and narrow, although a glass of red wine would, indeed, be good with lasagna. It's just that it's not worth it to me so I tell people simply, "No thank you, I already had my share for a life time."

Do I ever miss it? Of course. Alcohol is a social lubricant and at a cocktail party recently, I watched the people around me getting pleasantly talkative without becoming disgustingly sloshed. Instead of joining in, I remained the perpetually alert designated driver. I suspect that my indulgence in ice cream is literally a cold comfort that serves some of the same purposes that alcohol used to. I also figured out that wine was immensely appealing to me aesthetically, looking at the different colors and glass bottles with the light refracting through them. (I began collecting kaleidoscopes instead to satisfy that passion for translucent color.) I used to read about addictions and how they're often a wrong way to try to get to a right outcome. For some reason, I was struck by the image of trying to hammer a nail in with a high heeled shoe. Does it work? Yes, to some extent, but not as well, never as well, as a hammer. Nothing is ultimately as intoxicating as freedom.

Rezelations are the perfect joining of desire and action. I'm not sure they can be planned or willed into being but I am certain that having a family and a community to be responsible for gives a reason for life-affirming behavior. May you keep your New Year's resolutions—and may you find your own rezelations!

(January 1999)

Yardsticks

Instead of making those fragile and frustrating resolutions, this year I'm going to go with a new approach: yardsticks. I have a couple of key phrases that I've pondered and my plan is to use them to measure my thoughts, words and actions.

The first is the Arts and Crafts designer William Morris' question, "Is it beautiful? Is it useful?" He urged people—and I mean, long before feng shui became popular!—to toss out clutter. Victorians were the first beneficiaries of the Industrial Revolution's outpouring of cheaply manufactured goods. Morris looked at windows swathed in six layers of draperies as well as other icons of middle class respectability, then asked, what is enough? Could the eye perhaps be better pleased with a single pattern than a room run riot with color? Could the soul find more joy in a single well-loved object of beauty rather than a shelf of bric-a-brac? It was with that thought in mind that I weeded out my urban sprawl of miniature cottages and yes, even the ceramic poodles. I wasn't brave enough to get rid of anything just yet, but I boxed up a lot of it, leaving only what seemed truly delightful when I looked at it.

As for the other half of the question, "Is it useful?" there's the wonderful phrase I've mentioned before, "It might be useful One Day is the enemy of Today." Look into your own utility drawer in your kitchen and tell me if you're ready to part with that roll of string, that plastic switch plate. The only absolute certainty is that you'll need it as soon as it's gone. Nonetheless, the yardstick comes out to gauge whether a third broom is really needed, even if two definitely are.

My second measurement: "Is it truthful? Is it kind?" There are often times when it's tempting to blurt out something that's absolutely, undeniably true—but is it also kind? Even after I factor in my "but it's for your own good" intentions, can I claim that my basic motivation is kindness?

That goes beyond the idea of saying something nice or not at all, because niceness can sometimes be tainted with a desire to please which is at odds with honesty. Tact and respect really do go a long way toward making good decisions about how to communicate. Eastern religions have a concept which roughly translates as lovingkindness although Christians might term it agape. It takes effort to remember to address the struggling soul that lives inside each person, and not just the sometimes unappealing exterior. But hey, where would the sport be if it were easy??

In the average year, I read dozens of books on psychology, spirituality, self-help and other topics. The theme that comes through time and again is that the universe where we live inside our own skulls is also what we see around us. "The world is not as it is, but as we are," runs a saying. There's even a theory that when we slip free of our bodies, heaven or hell will depend on the contents of our own minds and hearts. My, that can be sobering when I find myself gnawing on an old grudge. I stop and ask myself whether that's how I'd like to spend eternity, or if it might be worthwhile to focus on more positive thoughts. I fall short of the ideal routinely, but it still seems worth the effort to strive for what is good and joyous in life.

As the recent series of articles in the Springfield *State Journal-Register* showed, there are various opinions about Enos Park held by both residents and people who live outside our area. "It's horrible," says one. "It's paradise," says another. For ten years, I've watched the neighborhood struggle back one day at a time. I'm delighted with the turnout for the Christmas Historic House Tour and with the great PR in the newspaper—such praise is hard-earned and overdue. We owe so much to so many but most of all to Marilyn Piland for her devotion. (Whenever I hear the idiom about someone having enough energy to run a small city, I smile to think of how many square blocks Marilyn routinely powers up on sheer will and gumption.)

Choose your own yardsticks to measure yourself against, and then find how much you've grown by the end of 2002. Happy New Year to all!

(January 2002)

Spring in Springfield

There I was today, parked outside the Schnucks at Montvale while the rain came down. Big fluffy raindrops at the end of April, drops that were giving serious thought to becoming sleet. The daffodils were lying with their heads down on the brick planter, whimpering, "This isn't right!" The only comfort was the certainty that a month into official spring, this can't last forever. I remembered a quote, "Climate is what you expect; weather is what you get."

This same sort of day would seem bleak in October, a first taste of months to come of cold and dark, though there might also be the cozy promise of a fireplace to offset the gloom. As it is, arriving after the taxes are in, it's an oddity to be endured, like the year we hunted undyed Easter eggs in the snow. (My spell-checker just flagged "undyed" and suggested "undead" which leads me to believe it doesn't know much about the usual tone of children's Easter egg hunts.) Soon enough, we'll be seeing more flesh than we really care to at Schnucks as central Illinoisans strip off everything they think they can get away with for the July swelter.

My first truly conscious thought came when I was perhaps three years old while curled beneath the kitchen table in a forest of chrome legs. I was thinking to myself that it was summer again and I remembered when it was summer before. My fascination with the wheel of the year hasn't dimmed. My mother often told me of a similar but more cosmic moment she'd had as a wee girl while sitting under lilacs in Arkansas: "I have always been, I will always be," she thought to herself in rapt amazement.

We all face the prospect of death but we are not all equally sure of annihilation. Some people think it's like a switch turned off, blink, they just don't exist any more. (Where does the candle flame go when you blow it out?) There. Not there. There. Not there. We pop into and out of life like an existential game of peek-a-boo. Some people have religious faith or spiritual philosophy to explain what happens when the breath and body part company. Despite some fabulous rewards offered for proof positive from the Other Side, no one has as yet been able to collect on them.

I've been pondering this of late as the reality sets in that parents are not as young as they used to be. Middle age means chats in the women's room about capital gains, pillow talk about deferred compensation and phone calls for health updates. I've joined one of those societies one really doesn't want to be a member of: the "How's Your Dad Doing?" club. How did time slip up on us girlfriends so that the topic isn't cute boys but ailing fathers? Kim's dad is in an oxygen tent, Eileen's passed away, Cynthia's is ailing and Karen's father barely manages to totter around his garden.

My own dad, Hal, is trailing an oxygen tank and has a new career lecturing smokers about what they're doing to their lungs even as he wheezes past the fibers that built up in his from decades of cigarettes. It's nerve-wracking to watch pounds fall off him until he looks like a leaf in the wind but it's part of the cycle of age. It's in the season of things that 75 isn't 25. I hope the medicines will help and that he'll regain his appetite, then his strength. I hope it with all my heart.

I'll say this for my Dad, he's like a lion in winter, still managing to roar. He's taking flying lessons as a continuation of his life-long habit of seizing the day and throttling it. "Make your lemons into lemonade!" has been his rallying cry down through the years, even when citrus seemed to arrive by the truckload.

Middle age means giving up illusions of invulnerability. Each day becomes more precious than the last as we comprehend that the supply is limited. The wheel of the year turns and we hear its creaking in our joints. But for all that, it's a time of life far sweeter than any that's come before. Love and laughter mixed with tears makes a tasty lemonade after all.

(May 1999)

~TRAVEL~

Key West

I suppose other people have done it, too—gone off to a motel in a distant city to do things you'd never dream of engaging in when you're at your own home. You know, get a little wild and crazy, live out a few fantasies, why not?

My version of that is to be scrupulously neat. A housekeeper coming into my hotel room may find all my cosmetics and toiletries lined up in a row of descending height, and color-coordinated to boot. My few items are neatly hung or folded in drawers whereas our home tends to chaos, not fastidious order. I believe in minimalist packing because one of the best bits of advice I ever encountered was, "When traveling, take half as many clothes as you think you'll need and twice as much money."

I'm not a contingency packer. When heading for Britain I don't have an outfit suitable for tea with the Queen because if I get invited, I can buy something for the occasion in London. Kevin and I wash out clothing in sinks or even at local Laundromats where we've met some charming locals. We're also reasonably certain that people in the next town won't exclaim in horror, "Good heavens! Didn't that woman have on the same black skirt yesterday?" (My husband's sisters took seven changes of clothing for a one week trip; our neighbor Jeff took 12 pairs, count 'em, a dozen khaki shorts with him to China.) No, the best bet is to travel light, in part because you never know when you'll have to lug the bag around for hours.

Kevin and I spent St. Patrick's Day weekend in Key West this year and we did indeed have to carry our luggage while taking the trolley tour because our host at the B&B wasn't in when we arrived. Key West is the southernmost city in the United States, the last wag of the tail of the Florida Keys. It gave me a whole new appreciation for spring and early summer as a run-up to our brutal Illinois summers because that gives us chance to adjust. As it was, we left gray, cold winter and stepped into a heat index of over 90 degrees, with blistering sun and humidity that reminded me of State Fair weather. I developed new respect for the wise people who invented siestas, sleeping away the hottest part of the day under shelter, then coming out at night when tropical breezes live up to their reputation.

It was also spring break which is the reason we chose to go then since Kevin teaches part-time at Lincoln Land and I'm on the adjunct faculty at University of Illinois at Springfield. However, that also meant that thousands of drunken students were swilling green beer and wearing rude T-shirts, spilling out of the bars all along lower Duval Street. "If I were 22, this would look like a lot of fun," mused my husband. Instead, we dodged students as they zipped around on scooters in a sort of Irish Mardi Gras frenzy.

What did I pack to bring back to Enos Park from this trip? Skip the tourist souvenirs, what's really worth taking away from an eight mile square island that looms so large in people's minds as a paradise on earth? Aside from climate, what have they got that makes their tiny frame houses go for $350,000?

The town is clean and filled with energy, enthusiasm, excitement, plus a sense of its own magic. For example, they've turned sunset into a big production every evening at Mallory Square and folks, it's the SAME sun we've got here! But they've done a better job of getting people from all over the planet to come to see it set in Key West. They make it seem like a privilege to be in their town, and a luxury to live there. Think about that. And keep it in mind when you talk to others about Enos Park because if we don't believe it's wonderful, why should they? We have a lot to be proud of and to share.

Now if only we could get Jimmy Buffet to sing "Cheeseburger at Suzie-Q's" we'd have it made.

(April 2001)

Davenport

"Drop everything" is usually just a turn of phrase, but there are conferences where I do just that, in order to fling myself into the arms of colleagues who've become friends over the past decade. Once a year those of us who work on statewide career information systems in the Midwest get together and what a joy it is! These are people who know *exactly* what it's like to head off for parts unknown with a vague map and a satchel full of handouts to do training at some remote high school or college. They, too, have discovered that the lab that was supposed to have Internet access is actually filled with Apple IIe relics. We're all quite clear from coping with others' networks that "when it comes to computers, Murphy was an optimist."

This year's conference was at the end of April in Davenport, Iowa. I enjoyed accidentally taking the longcut to my destination because it meant that I had a chance to see even more homes built along the Mississippi bluffs in the Quad Cities area. Some were original Arts & Crafts, Queen Anne, Tudor Revival and Italianate, others were more recent ranches and mountain chalet designs. Along the riverfront of Davenport there's an area called East Village filled with historic buildings housing small shops, ice cream parlors and even a combination bike rental/espresso bar. The actual downtown a few blocks away reminded me of Joliet. It had much the same vintage commercial buildings with a mix of surviving shops and empty storefronts hanging on until the next promised wave of economic development from casinos.

The Blackhawk Hotel where the conference was held was built in 1915 and is on the National Register of Historic Places—beautiful ironwork on the railings, but alas, no task lighting or data ports in the rooms. Nonetheless, it was a very pleasant place to stay. I woke in the wee hours of morning to the rumble of a train over a nearby trestle and listened to the whistles of barges on the river before sliding back into sleep. (When we lived on 4th Street, the tracks were only inches away from our garage and I learned to snooze through Amtrak trains rolling past.) Earlier in the evening, the view from the restaurant on the 11th floor had been entrancing, golden lights reflecting on the black waters of the Mississippi.

What I admire about Davenport—and for that matter, Dubuque, Galena and St. Charles—is the way each has capitalized on what it has to offer as a river city with a history that's worth keeping. The buildings have been preserved and used for many purposes throughout the years. And I ask you, what's not to love about painted ladies tricked out in their gaudy coats of paint and flouncing their verandas? Well-tended structures make a statement that someone cares, and like my long-term friendships with colleagues, that people have put in the effort to sustain and improve them over the years.

Despite the Sangamon, no one would call Springfield a river town, that's not our identity. We have to look for something else to promote and the most obvious feature is our favorite son, Abraham Lincoln. As the new presidential library takes shape, we have an opportunity for Enos Park to be part of the worldwide interest that will be focused on Springfield. Kevin had a brilliant idea: make 6th Street a virtual river, a corridor from the museum to Oak Ridge Cemetery, where tourists can flow. Make sure each building along the route is a showplace, not an eyesore (and to be honest, some are in poor condition). Though several owners and developers are already well along the way on rehabbing homes and putting up new condos, we need everyone on board for a project of this magnitude.

Let's create a 6th Street Historic Corridor so that the entire route is a source of civic pride as the world comes to visit the places where Lincoln walked. Enos Park has an opportunity to do something wonderful to both support the city of Springfield and to enchant the millions of visitors who will travel through here in the decades to come.

(May 2002)

Pacific Northwest

It was the roach in the bathtub that tore it. I was willing to overlook the dirty carpet, the chest of drawers that Goodwill would scorn, and even the bare light bulb in the ceiling fixture. But when I tried to wash the bug down the drain and water came out of the tap as brown as weak coffee, I decided no, this would not do.

We were in Seaside, "the resort capital of Oregon," and decided to try something different than a chain motel, something with a bit of local color. The Driftwood looked delightful from the outside, each lavender guest cottage painted with ivy vines. My theory was that it would be decorated even more charmingly inside. Wrong. The manager desperately wanted to keep the $37.45 that Kevin had already given her, so she moved us up to the special deluxe unit at no extra charge. (It had the added benefit of being farther away from the screaming couple next to the first room.) This one was meant for long-term stays, with a kitchenette furnished with both a hotplate and a tiny refrigerator. The curtains were hand-made and there was a little plastic table and chair set and even paper doilies. I still wouldn't step into the shower but the TV worked and the bed was free of vermin—which was more than could be said of a bed & breakfast with fleas in Boston. "At one time, families came here and thought it was a very nice place," Kevin reminded me but I had visions of men nowadays renting the room by the week while plying the "Will Work for Food" trade.

All in all, it made for an amusing contrast to Port Townsend, Washington where we'd stayed at Manressa Castle the night before. That's a turreted Victorian extravaganza built by an industrialist in the town's heyday, before the bad news that the railroad was going to Seattle instead. It was a prosperous area fallen on times so hard no one had the money to tear down the buildings. Lovely confections of ornamented stone still line their main street which has become a thriving tourist destination. Perhaps too much so—the local paper was singing the woes of rapid development, insufficient infrastructure and all those dreadful people moving in and changing the place with their citified ways. As so often happens, the earlier immigrants want to close the door behind themselves and keep newcomers out. Some of their complaints are valid such as speeding tourists on the roads, strip malls springing up in the shadow of glistening white lighthouses, rent skyrocketing for long time residents. But with the ferries and highways, it's now possible to commute to jobs in Seattle while living on the islands or the Olympic Peninsula. Why settle for a coffee from Starbucks when you can stop at Fred's Espresso and Fish Bait by a logging camp on your way to work?

Some years back, I was whining at a party that Kevin wouldn't take me where I wanted to go for my birthday. Dee, a rather formidable woman, whirled on Kevin and began berating him. He took it for a while and then said, "Dee, she wants to go to Seattle." "Oh, I thought she wanted to go to Red Lobster," she gasped, abashed for perhaps the first time in her life. Well, we didn't make it to the Pacific Northwest in 1992 but we have twice since then. Kevin's birthday is in August and he's holding out for Milwaukee for his trip.

He was thrilled with the harbor tour in Bremerton of the mothball fleet. They had the Triton submarine that was the first to circle the globe completely underwater. A wide variety of boats and ships were on their way to becoming razor blades and Chevrolets, the guide told us. He gave statistics about the number of people who serve on aircraft carriers, each large enough to have its own zip code with twice the population of the town where Kevin grew up.

Odd. Whether we're looking at floating cities or artist colonies, tourist towns or major metropolitan areas, we're always asking questions about how people live in the structures they create. There's an ebb and flow to the way people decide what's desirable real estate and what's not. Maybe that's why year after year, Kevin and I watch with delight as Enos Park is gradually restored to its place as a favorite neighborhood in Springfield.

(August 1999)

San Francisco

Kevin had a wonderful time in San Francisco last month; as is so often the case, he was able to go along with me on my business trip. I'd spend from 8 a.m. until 6:30 p.m. at my conference, cooped up in a basement meeting room at the hotel. By the end of the day, my idea of a hot night on the town was ordering pizza in to our room and watching re-runs on TV. He, on the other hand, enjoyed breakfasting on croissants at a local coffee shop, strolling through town, looking at boats tied up at the pier and generally having a jolly good time. One day he rented a recumbent bicycle and rode across the Golden Gate Bridge then took the ferry back from Sausalito. Frankly, I was envious. But that's the sort of thing I should have expected as part and parcel of winning the War of Liberation I fought for as a women's studies major in my college days. I get to work while my spouse plays in the sunshine, I get to pump my own gas in windswept northern Illinois stations as I drive around on business. I won—I think.

We did get out a little together to explore the city by the bay. For example, one evening we took a cab across town to a used bookstore. The taxi driver who picked us up asked us what we were doing there. "Well, shopping for books," we said, puzzled, what else? He said in 18 years as a cabbie, this was the first time he'd ever picked up someone from a bookstore. At that rate, he would have been aghast by my idea of a Saturday free in San Francisco—I mapped out a route to cover as many book and kaleidoscope shops as possible. We took a cable car into the center of the city from our Fisherman's Wharf hotel, and I quite cheerfully avoided the Chinese New Year parade for a chance to dig through a few more shops. Kevin was reasonably good, he didn't get surly until after the first half dozen. (And he claims he was mostly peeved by walking 10 blocks at night in a questionable neighborhood. Tsk, tsk. But I found a 1978 out-of-print paperback on my want list so I considered it effort well spent.) We tromped up hills and down hills enough to make me deeply sad that I've gotten so out of shape over the winter.

Haight-Ashbury was the time capsule we'd imagined it would be. As we drove past the painted lady row houses, we saw girls with long hair parted down the middle who were wearing earth mother dresses and pounding on drums, swaying to the music on the steps of one. "Does the National Park Service pay them to do this?" we asked locals. Heck, where we come from, Lincoln impersonators are a dime a dozen and many people dress up as seemingly authentic New Salem residents, albeit with much better teeth. The Haight was not as shabby as I'd imagined it would be. Apparently, real estate is far too expensive to let it run down. There were still day-glo VW microbuses, we saw at least four. It's a mecca for the Deadheads and for all the counter-culture aging hippies. Still, there were quite a few of the punk and grunge variety of kids mixed in as well.

We'd sit on the city bus and point out turrets and windows and clever paint combinations to each other. The riot of color makes me wish more than ever for more seminars in Springfield on "The Art of the Painted Lady." White foursquare houses simply don't have the same panache as gingerbread picked out in three or four shades. That was something we always loved about our house on Fourth Street: the white and blue color scheme with the blueberry trim. When Habitat for Humanity did the one next door, it was obvious that someone knew and enjoyed putting colors together, too, and it made ours look sedate by comparison.

Housing prices there are astronomical and parking is abysmal. Going away is fun but coming home is always better. I found I had no desire to leave my heart in San Francisco—it's firmly anchored here in the Midwest, strung along I-55 from Springfield to Mt. Olive to St. Louis.

(April 1996)

London

Chestnuts actually *were* roasting on an open fire in a cart next to the British Museum. We'd read advice to tourists that warned, "they smell better than they taste" so we passed by them. Night falls even sooner in England than it does here and by 4 p.m. it was getting dark. We walked several blocks and finally found the Waterstone's bookstore in an old building with turrets, nooks, crannies and window seats. And what delights there were within!

Kevin and I went to England in November on what we call the 2001 Books and Brew Tour. He had his list of pubs that serve real ale, and I had my carefully chosen bookstores. Our friend Steve is teaching history at Canterbury Christ Church College this semester and he was delighted when we took him up on his invitation to hop the pond to visit. As usual, we tried to see and do too much instead of relaxing so we got to London, Cambridge, Greenwich, Canterbury and York. Much of the trip was a blur of transfers between trains, the Underground tube, escalators, a boat on the Thames, buses, taxies, express shuttles and even a monorail. Much as I enjoyed Charing Cross Road's book sellers, I was happy to get away from the crowds of London by the time we arrived at Steve's temporary home in Canterbury.

Our bed and breakfast was in a 13th century building that escaped the ravages of heavy bombing during World War II. The famous cathedral also survived, as did some of the buildings from the time of Chaucer's *Canterbury Tales*. One church has been in continuous use since about 600 A.D. There was something magical about wandering dark twisty little streets and peering into shop windows lit like treasure boxes both there and in York. We watched men stringing Christmas lights in the trees and we lunched at an inn where weavers made cloth centuries before Columbus thought he'd found a quick route to India. Ceilings were low and dark with heavy beams, glass was wavy with age. It made a wonderful contrast to the trendy department store windows in London where computer controlled light displays spelled out messages about buy, buy, buy. (See, they're also being urged to shop though not as a patriotic duty to bail out the economy as we are.)

"Americans are thin on the ground these days," observed one bookstore owner. Indeed, we ran into very few—we ourselves were often mistaken for Brits and asked for directions. Yet invariably, as soon as people identified us as being from the States, they offered condolences for the recent events. "We'll do for that Dust Bin Laden, we will!" proclaimed a chap at the Eight Bells Pub, then laughed uproariously at his own joke: dustbin is the English term for trashcan. People we met were unfailingly kind and supportive, eager to aid the war on terrorism.

So, we now have memories of Jolly Olde England dressed up for the holidays, from glam-rock mannequins in Harrod's windows to paper bells and streamers at a tea shop in an ancient chapel in York. Nice enough, all of it, but we were ready to come home to see our own history, even though it's less than two centuries old in Springfield. EPNIA's first-ever Holiday House Tour will be filled with light and scent and color enough to make us proud.

We'll keep our holiday traditions and form new ones such as the Christmas Closet boutique. We hope to see you on December 8 from noon until 4 p.m. at some of the eight houses on the tour. They'll vary in their restoration progress and their architectural style; I doubt that our buildings will still be standing in the year 3001, but who knows? The builders in Canterbury and York weren't thinking of their structures lasting as long as they have, either. Somebody must have taken care of them in the meantime. That's a wonderful gift that we can all give to ourselves and our homes in the years to come.

(December 2001)

Galena

It's the fall training season again and I'll have a busy schedule traveling around the state of Illinois for the next several months. It's ironic, in a way, that I drive so much for my job. As a child, I learned to despise long car trips but of course the view from the back seat wasn't as interesting as it is from behind the wheel. When young we're at the mercy of adults to decide not only the destination and route, but basics such as when to pull off the highway. It was a wretched thing that I both loved to read and hated to ride in the car, but couldn't read in the car without getting nauseated. Being grown up means I can stop where I please and even enjoy books on tape during the four hours to Chicago.

One of the perks of my job is getting to drive through small towns and look at the variety of ways that people live. Often the two lane highways go through town squares and the roads are lined with the Victorian houses of the local gentry. "Hmm, somebody was sure well-to-do," I think, as I admire turrets and gingerbread or elaborate masonry on wrap-around porches. Often, the nicest houses in town have been converted to funeral parlors (as the Ferguson House was here in Springfield), giving the departed a last, grand send-off. Others now serve as bed and breakfasts or country inns, capitalizing on their areas' antique shops and atmosphere far from the gritty urban streets.

Of course, not everything in the country is automatically an improvement over city living. I also drive by tumbled down houses that don't look fit for human habitation that nonetheless have laundry fluttering on lines outside and probably more dogs under the porch than the county pound. Some towns have the boarded-up look of despair and it doesn't take much imagination to figure out why the kids would want to pack up and jump a Greyhound as soon as possible. While we deplore people not speaking to their neighbors in the city, there's nonetheless something to be said for the privacy it affords. Anonymity can be a relief compared to local gossip. Small towns are terribly vulnerable to the loss of their economic base, too, whether it's farming, mining or a local business that decided to shut its doors.

Yet on the whole, I'm enchanted by the small towns with their diners and one pump gas stations, their tiny schools with a hundred students in K-12. As I drive on the interstates, I pick up radio stations running contests where the prize is 50 cents for a correct answer to a trivia question and I smile. Often there are community calendar spots to keep folks updated about the town council meeting, the volunteer firefighters, the quilters' group at the church. I'm just passing through, collecting memories of a barn here, a burst of autumn foliage there. Sometimes I take Kevin with me on my business trips and show him the places I've found.

That's how we came to love Galena so much. It's in the far northwest corner of the state and, like the Cotswolds of England, they were just too darn poor to pull their buildings down and put up new ones. Now it's a perfectly preserved village with the new development ringing it but not intruding upon it. It's gone from a backwater with real estate you could scarcely give away to a town with skyrocketing property values. Houses along the main street get snapped up for over $200,000 instead of the $20,000 they begged for a few years ago. They've had the sense to preserve what they have and to carefully capitalize on it. I doubt that people there claim that buildings "have no historic value" or "have lost all their integrity" just because they've been used for several purposes during the century. It adds, instead, a rich patina of human connection.

Will Enos Park be as smart? Can we have the best of small town living by bonding together as a community, yet with city amenities such as universities, hospitals, government and a variety of businesses? Will we have the sense to keep the best of the past while adding new features as needed? I have faith that we will.

(October 1996)

Galena Revisited

Being in love is such fun—the rush of adrenaline, the thrill…but sometimes it fades and I think I'm over it. Then I discover it's all still there, real and passionate as it ever was. How could I have thought that I'd ever be anything other than in love with Galena?

It's in the northwest corner of Illinois in an area that glaciers missed. I've grown used to the flat cornfields and prairie in the central part of the state, but something in me responds to the rolling hills up north. Past life memory? Perhaps. There's just something alluring about gazing across a valley with terraces in variegated colors, greens, russets and tans in a swirling patchwork, the hills beyond blued with atmospheric perspective.

There are scenic lookouts on Route 20 between Freeport and Dubuque where one can see a three-state area. "Be alert for crosswinds" warn road signs, and as I look over the drop, I shudder. Still, the outcroppings of rock on the bluffs looming above the Great River Road along Highway 84 are beautiful. We drove up through the Mississippi Palisades State Park and admired the 220,000-acre wildlife refuge. Eagles return to the same nests year after year and continue to expand them. Some reach up to 10 feet in diameter and can weigh several tons. Kevin said he could imagine other eagles sniffing disdainfully, "Hmmph. MacAeries." That made me laugh.

We found historic homes in Mt. Carroll that were beautiful: there was a Tudor Revival built in 1925 and several Victorians with cupolas, turrets, second floor porches, and vivid paint jobs. What a nice array of public buildings and residences they have at their county seat! It's also home to the Campbell Center for Historic Preservation, see http://www. campbellcenter.org. They offer classes and workshops on topics such as plaster repair, stabilizing historic buildings and conservation of collections. How often do we hear, "It was too far gone, we couldn't save it" as Springfield's heritage is torn down for yet another parking lot? This month it's the oldest Catholic church in town, it'll be something else before long. Oh boy, would I ever like to send some folks to the Campbell Center if I thought it'd do the least bit of good!

We first wandered into Galena in 1991. I've written in previous columns that it's an example of Cotswold Syndrome because they were too poor after the lead mine closed to tear down their buildings and put up new ones. Instead, it looks much as it did when Ulysses S. Grant and his family lived there. The main street curves gently and nearly every shop front is now filled with antiques and boutiques, restaurants and coffee-houses, local businesses and hotels. There's something magical about walking through cold, gray air and then entering shops, which are warm, well-lit, good smelling and filled with jeweled colors, twinkling stained glass and soft fabrics. Of course, we spent some dollars, too, on books, a carafe, and that wonderful cinnamon orange herbal tea that I brew as house scent. Although we didn't buy anything at the pottery gallery that's in a defunct brewery, we had a great conversation with the artist who's also a home brewer. Another time, he'd given Kevin a tour of the cellar where beer had been lagered and showed him the hop vines now growing wild behind the stone building.

Enos Park has genuine historic character, charm and a mix of businesses and residences. It's up to us to continue to cherish what's unique about our area. Once upon a time, Galena was run down, shabby and depressed. Now the problem is too much money pouring in and changing the character of the town from sleepy village to a Chicagoans' getaway resort. Well, as problems go, I think I'd like for us to try too much wealth, just for a change of pace, you understand.

And we can go on, year after year, being in love with Enos Park.

(November 2002)

~HUSBAND AND HOUNDS~

Kevin's Birthday

To me, coffee smells like love.

It's the scent of brewing coffee that pulls me downstairs in the morning because Kevin almost always gets to the kitchen first and starts it. The smell reminds me of all the cups of coffee he's bought for me from Edinburgh, Scotland, to San Francisco with a lot of points in between.

Aside from coffee, Kevin cooks a third of the time while restaurants and I handle the remainder. He enjoys scandalizing a macho young friend of his by buying cookbooks and enthusiastically using them. This is a guy who is truly secure in his masculinity: after all, he routinely parades around in public—quite literally!—wearing a skirt and purse, albeit with armed state troopers surrounding him doing the same thing. (They *prefer* to call it a kilt and a sporran.)

He has utterly no interest in sports and doesn't golf, fish or hunt. He not only puts the toilet seat down, he puts new rolls of paper in the holder. When he's gotten lost while driving, he didn't hesitate to pull into a filling station and ask for directions. Kevin enjoys shopping at the mall as much as he likes going to gun shows. When he's sick, he makes his own doctor's appointment and goes promptly; if it's bad enough for him to be a patient at home, he's considerate and grateful for being tended. He's remarkably clear on the concept that if something around the house bothers him, such as pet hair on the rugs, it's up to him to get out the vacuum and take care of it. The worst complaint I can come up with is that he often leaves socks he's worn on the floor next to his shoes rather than promptly putting them into the hamper.

Kevin likes all of his in-laws and they adore him in return. He has never, ever once forgotten my birthday or our anniversary and the presents he gives me are perfect because he asks me what I want. He's easy to buy for because of his varied interests in military history, aviation, computers, travel and gaming. (On Sunday afternoons his pals come over, swill homebrew and blast each other's miniature spaceships to hypothetical smithereens.)

He gets involved in lots of organizations including the Enos Park Neighborhood Improvement Association. He doesn't just join on paper, he goes to the meetings, serves on boards, volunteers and gets some of the unglamorous things done. He's happiest being one of those solid, salt of the earth types who keeps everything running smoothly behind the scenes. One of his unsung contributions is giving me feedback on these columns before I send them in. He laughs at all the right places and often has good ideas on how to improve them (except this one: I'm sneaking it in without him seeing it first!)

A man who can manage to be a hero to his own wife is an exceptional human being and there isn't a day that goes by that I don't silently thank Lela and Virgil Brown for raising such a fine son. The funny part is that when I first met him I thought, "Well, he's a nice guy but he's not my type." And, indeed, he was not the neurotic, artistic intellectual sort I was used to dating. He was a small town boy, a healthy, cheerful Navy veteran. It took a lot of getting used to. And although I'd like to win the lottery, I've accepted the fact that I may have used up my supply of luck against the odds by finding Kevin and having the sense to marry him. That's OK with me, because I won something far more valuable than mere millions.

Why am I telling you folks all this? Just to rub in the fact that Mrs. Mel Gibson probably sits up nights, gnashing her teeth in envy of me?

No, I'm offering it as an example of how private life can spill over into public action. A happy marriage is at the core of a harmonious family and then families link together into communities. When we are at peace with ourselves, we have the energy to turn outward and tackle issues, becoming part of the solution instead of part of the problem. Love that we feel for our families can be expanded into a love for the neighborhoods we call home.

The world is clearly a better place because Kevin is in it and Enos Park benefits from his skills, time and enthusiasm. I hope you'll join with me in wishing him a very happy birthday on the 28th of this month!

(August 1995)

Onward to Scotland

For obvious reasons, soon after the August column about Kevin appeared, I whisked him out of the country. My theory was that after a few weeks, women would decide that I was either joking or hallucinating about a man who *actually puts toilet paper on the roll* and that they would not be as likely to try to kidnap him. So we hid out in the highlands of Scotland until I was pretty sure it had all blown over.

Of course, the problem was that we became enchanted with Scotland in the process. We'd spent some time there in 1989 but this was two weeks of exploration from Edinburgh to Glasgow, then up the west coast to Oban and the Isle of Skye, then across through Inverness and down the east coast to Pitlochry, Perth and to Stirling in the center. We toured half a dozen castles and saw many more from the train. But worst of all, Kevin found a castle in the classified ads. There it was, for sale, doubtless a money pit of magnificent proportions.

I argued that we should win the lottery and then buy an advertised kirk (that's Gaelic for church) that had already been transformed into a residence. It was only an hour from Glasgow Airport, I pointed out, and had frills like central heating and electricity. But no, there was something about the idea of owning a real castle that appealed to my husband. Maybe it was the prospect of standing atop towers with parapets to play his pipes. Maybe it's the same quixotic passion which makes him long to buy and rehabilitate houses here in Springfield that might daunt Bob Villa or even make Norm think twice.

Me, I'd be quite content to buy a burned out croft and transport the stones to Illinois for a vacation cottage near Galena. I daresay they're pretty inexpensive by comparison because hundreds of roofless buildings dot the countryside as mute reminders of The Clearances. That was an era in the 1700s when the landowners decided that sheep were more profitable than farmers and they drove their tenants off the land. Ever wonder where the word "fired" comes from which so neatly rhymes with "hired"? The landowners set fire to the crofts as a way to make sure people got the message and didn't try to return to their homes where they'd lived on for generations.

The first wave of Scots who were deported to the New World went kicking and screaming. However, the land here was open and fertile and soon they were writing to relatives that the colonies and Canada weren't so bad. Getting people to board the boats for the second and third waves of clearances was a much simpler task.

While I regret the pain and upheaval in their lives, memorialized by those abandoned crofts, I think of the how expatriate Scots have made their mark all over the world, taking with them a rich cultural heritage. Around the planet, poet Robert Burns' birthday is celebrated each January with Scotch and haggis. (And if you don't know what haggis is, it's probably best to leave it that way—let's just say U.S. Customs has been known to refuse shipments of it as "unfit for human consumption.")

Change is hard, sometimes cruelly hard. When I look at development plans for Enos Park in the next decade, I notice some of it calls for clearances here, too. Rows of gleaming townhouses are proposed but that would mean tearing down buildings that may be dearly loved by the people who live there now. I drive up and down the blocks, trying to imagine what it would mean to the current residents. Would they be thrilled? Dismayed? Would it be a windfall for them? Would Enos Park keep its unique historical character while also incorporating new residential and commercial developments?

At this point, it's nothing more than a lot of questions. As Mark Gordon at Historic Sites put it so succinctly, we don't want to destroy Enos Park in the process of trying to preserve it. We want to plan for the best possible elements which will retain the charm of Enos Park while adding to its vitality. We shall settle for no less.

(October 1995)

Marriage

We were out having dinner with friends and their 19-year-old son. He announced proudly, "I've got my opinions set, and I don't need any role models." I thought we did well, hiding our smiles in our napkins instead of just guffawing in his face. I was thinking, "Enjoy it while you can, kiddo, because you'll never again be as certain that you know it all as you do when you're under 20."

Me, I'm 46 and have to constantly review and revise my opinions. Kevin and I have lots of role models and one of our favorites is Mary Worth.

Not everyone likes the cartoon strip as much as we do. In a recent Springfield *State Journal-Register*, an irate letter writer claimed that, thanks to continental drift, his mother, dead and buried in her grave since 1985, had progressed more than Mary Worth during that same period. Clearly he had not actually been following the strip or he would have known that story lines usually take a couple of months to evolve, then they change to a new entanglement. (I sometimes wonder about Mary's screening criteria since she allows such an odd assortment of characters to move into the Charterstone Apartments that she manages.) We eagerly read the strip for the expression on faces, sometimes outlandishly more emotional than the situation seems to call for: "Ian! The *doorbell*!!!"

Kevin and I continue to burn with desire to know how Toby ended up married to Professor Cameron. It happened before our time and they're an odd couple, she a slender young blonde and he an older, gruff sea captain type. Must have made for an interesting courtship. Currently, Mary is being wooed by Jeff, a doctor who may have a drinking problem, while Jeff's son Drew is interested in a houseguest of Mary's who we suspect of being up to no good. Often people aren't what they seem upon closer inspection, or they find new sides of themselves, as did the tomboyish Will who traded in her boondockers for a life of true love and motherhood as Willow. Mary patiently doles out common sense and kindness to all comers, just as she has since 1939.

From the vantage point of a happy marriage, I can watch the scrambles of our real-world single friends with a sort of bemused horror. Their lives go through soap opera gyrations, too. I remember what it was like to be alone and to wonder whether I'd ever meet The One so I hope that the advice I'm providing is up to Mary Worth's standards. I've given away more than a dozen copies of Judith Sill's book *How to Stop Looking for Someone Perfect and Find Someone to Love*. I carefully charted the qualities I wanted most in a partner and discovered my healthiest relationships had been with men I'd admired and loved as friends. I just hadn't connected that there was anything romantic about trust, patience and kindness. From Sill's book I learned to let go of ideas about "my type" because what I wanted most might come in a different wrapper than I was expecting.

This turned out to be exactly true. Kevin is not my type. He's not a thin, lonely, artist with low self-esteem but a big, strapping lad with a cheerful disposition. He brought a dowry of friends to our marriage, stretching back to his childhood. To my amazement, I discovered that equal partnerships are a whole lot more fun than social work projects.

Listen up, out there! If you'd like to spend next Valentine's Day with someone special, use your reformer zeal on neighborhood improvement instead of focusing on yourself or trying to fix someone else because a) they don't appreciate it and b) it doesn't work. If you think that all the good ones are taken, they probably got snapped up while working on a Habitat for Humanity house. And trust me, finding The One is, indeed, worth the effort.

(February 2000)

Love and Community

"Do you two try to be disgusting, or does it just work out that way?"

No one's been quite that blunt, but that's the gist of the question: can Kevin and I really be that blitheringly adoring after so long together? Obviously, the answer is yes. We are guilty as charged of public displays of affection. Kevin remains the rarest of men, one who is a hero to his own wife.

In honor of Valentine's Day, I'm pondering the hearts in playing cards. Older still are the tarot cards where Cups symbolize emotions, feelings and relationships. The tarot has four suits, Cups, Swords, Wands and Coins which correspond to Hearts, Spades, Clubs and Diamonds. In addition, there are 22 cards in the major arcana, or the greatest mysteries, that show the journey of life. I got my first deck in high school and have remained fascinated ever since. I rarely read for others but use tarot as a tool for insight and reflection as the cards form an ever-changing kaleidoscope of possibilities.

People may see the Lovers card and think it refers to grand passions but it really doesn't, it has to do with making choices based on spiritual principles. For human scale love, it's the Two of Cups that one would hope for in a reading. It shows the stage of being enraptured with one another, where all the world can be found in the eyes of one's beloved. How delightful that is, young love at any age! Kevin and I carpool, we e-mail back and forth through the day, we call each other and sometimes go to lunch. We collaborate on whatever projects The Lucas Brown Partnership has going. Then in the evening we curl up on the couch with our pets. (Sleeping is a challenge with Kevin on one side of me and our 120 lbs. of dogs on the other, all trying to meet in the middle. Rolling over is a major accomplishment.)

The artwork on decks varies, but the Three of Cups card often shows three women with upraised goblets. That reminds me of friendships, of evenings when Kathy and Christa and I get together for chick flics and all the chocolate we care to eat. Women don't have corsets to unlace, hair pins to remove or high heels to kick off these days, but there's still a luscious sensation of relaxing with the girls. I've always liked the line, "Remember when jokes that couldn't be told in mixed company...weren't?" Well, they can be told when it's just us. I'm happy, too, when Kevin goes off to beer festivals with the guys because getting away for a while also means having the fun of coming back together.

But it's the Ten of Cups that's the most relevant to Enos Park. That has a happy couple under a rainbow arch of ten goblets signifying love in the context of community. Mature love has the muscle to tackle projects because it has reached a stage of generating something beyond itself. Sometimes that purpose takes the form of children to continue families. For those of us without children—by choice or by chance—there are other ways of touching the future: teaching, being aunts and uncles, befriending and mentoring youngsters. If they were dances, the Two of Cups would be Cinderella and the prince at the ball while the 10 of Cups would be a folk dance where the whole village does reels and polkas in the town square during a festival.

It's enchanting to think of children, teens, adults and elders joining hands in a huge circle around our neighborhood. The Spring Festival in the Park has a similar feel to it. That would be the Ace of Cups, a chalice brimming with love, light and hope.

If the truth be known, the best way to predict the future is to invent it. Nonetheless, Madame Lola foresees a wonderful 21st century for Enos Park—it's in the cards!

(February 2001)

Banking Points

Isn't banking rather an odd topic for a Valentine's Day column? Not if you have a lot invested in a relationship.

Long ago I read that the 80/20 rule applies in human interactions. Basically, that means that you need four positives for every negative just to stay even. People have a survival instinct that makes pain more vivid in experience and memory than pleasure, so it takes more to counterbalance hurts. Oh, and they do rack up, even in the best of friendships and marriages. We all get grouchy at times or find we've done something inconsiderate.

So if the ratio is 4:1, then the trick is to not only meet that but to exceed it. For Kevin and me, it's an on-going challenge to see how many points we can bank to stay ahead of the game. We don't keep literal count as we did when Saab Spotting was a highly competitive sport, but we do have a general idea of what's worth extra points. For example, routine household tasks earn credits: laundry, loading the dishwasher, taking out trash, mowing the lawn. Kevin got additional points for dragging holiday decorations from the basement, assembling the tree and putting up indoor and outdoor lights this year, pretty much by himself because I was tired from so much work-related travel. It wasn't glamorous but I fixed the slow bathtub drain. Our plumber-recommended standby of cider vinegar and bleach didn't help, so I took the strainer off and pulled out the accumulated gunk. Ewwww—but I got a lot of respect and gratitude from Kevin for tackling it. Truly, a dirty job but somebody had to do it.

Getting extra points from being a doting wife while shopping works, too. Just this morning Kevin mentioned the supply of instant soups that I'd picked up for him to keep at his office. Remembering to fetch what he asks for at the grocery is good for routine points; finding something to delight him, such as a chipotle raspberry marinade, is worth bonus points. I get a thrill out of tracking down obscure books, videos and music that he had despaired of ever locating. He in turn emerged from a store recently with a wedge of Irish cheese for me since he knows I'm part mouse. Seldom does he come home from a solo trip without a gift to show he was thinking of me. (I have to be very careful about what I express an interest in, because he'll go out of his way to obtain it for me. What can I say, I like that in a man.)

Early on, Kevin figured out that I could be lured into all sorts of things by the promise, "It'll be an adventure!" and then consoled afterwards, in some cases, by "Well, at least we'll get a good story out of this." We recently dined at a Vietnamese restaurant where we had to have things on the menu explained to us, and then we needed instructions on how to assemble the food they brought to the table. I'd never wrapped lettuce around an egg roll before! So he accumulated some bonus points for suggesting that we try something new.

I've written about Kevin being an outstanding husband. In the interests of fairness I should point out that I'm not a slouch as a wife. Just leaving the car to go into work each morning, he gets more of a send-off than some guys do going to war. After 14 years of knowing him, I'm still starry-eyed. Not to brag but as a statement of fact, I seem to have a considerable capacity for long-term devotion and adoration. We haven't kept count, but I'd guess the ratio of good to bad in our marriage is about 50:1.

In our kitchen is a framed Mary Engelbreit card that reads, "There is no more lovely, friendly and charming relationship, communion or company than a good marriage." That about covers it. Even when we're frazzled and irritable or at odds—and it does happen—I keep in mind that above and beyond all else, Kevin is my dearest friend in the world, just as I am his. We're not perfect, just perfect for each other.

Love helps us get beyond the pain and the inevitable rough spots of life. It's equally true of the love we have for our homes here in Enos Park. If you make it a game to see how many positives you can put back into the neighborhood for every negative that you encounter, you'll find yourself happier by far. Investing in our community provides wonderful dividends and the sum total of joy increases over the years. Monetary property values? Yes, those too, but best of all are the bonus points you'll bank from seeing Enos Park return to being the pride of Springfield.

(February 2003)

Fiona

When we came out of the convenience store there was a woman waiting. "I just had to see who belonged to the white standard poodle in your car," she greeted us. Before long we were over at her van being introduced to her black standard. After she drove off, I said to Kevin, "Egads, I feel like we just bought a Volkswagen."

And it's true, standard poodle people seem to instantly bond with each other like the legendary VW drivers. There's a black and white pair and a chocolate one who frequent Washington Park, and all their owners are quite talkative with Kevin. It delights us to see the smiles that Fiona gets from joggers, children, or people in cars and the way she gaily laughs back at them. She's brought incredible joy to our lives—watching her leap and run in the backyard gives me the same sensation as watching Olympic gymnasts: how does she *do* that? She has such grace, elegance, speed and strength as she twirls, bounds and cavorts.

We adopted Fiona in late September, thanks to our niece who volunteers at Adopt-a-Pet in Benld. We'd told Phyllis that we hoped to find a black standard poodle by fall. "Well, one's coming in," she reported. "Her people are getting a divorce and moving to apartments so she needs a home—but she may not be black. Why don't you come on down and take a look at her and see what you think?" I have one of those 'snapshots of the heart' of the moment I first glimpsed her, vividly white, running at dusk in a fenced area. I felt a lot of trepidation, though, as she jumped wildly around on the leash. At only 14 months old, she had megawatts of energy to burn. Once in the car she settled down and rode home on my lap. She was the size of Justin, yet she was also a white poodle like Tiny, the miniature I grew up with. With my arms around her, I fell in love before we even got on the highway to return to Springfield.

Being in love is sometimes embarrassing, of course. It means burbling excitedly to anyone I can corner about the remarkable Fiona and what new clever things she's done. It means carrying pictures of her in my purse and mailing them to friends. It's enriched pet supply stores as I buy special food, toys and accessories. "But Kevin, she *needs* a new Frisbee and a tuggy toy and a yellow plastic porcupine and another ball and…well, yes, and a nice plush orthopedic bed for her crate…" Fortunately, Kevin is as besotted as I am with the hound, which is a darn good thing because adjustment to an active, curious dog after years with an elderly one isn't easy. We've had to toddler-proof the house from her inquisitive mouth and paws. The cats have the worst of it because Fiona wants to play and they most emphatically do *not*.

Our vet, Dr. Paul McGowan, assures us that by the time she turns two, she'll be a dignified, responsible dog. As it is, she's a smart willful adolescent so Fiona and I enrolled in a training class where she quickly learned to walk on the leash—and to shake hands—in a ladylike manner. Going to school on Monday nights is a treat for both of us.

I think of Fiona's former owners often and with gratitude. Barbara was kind enough to send Fiona's puppy pictures which I wanted to see but wouldn't have dared to hope for. Each time I look at them, I think how loved that little dog is by so many people. Yes, she's rambunctious and no matter how often I brush her, she ends up looking like a ragamuffin. And we're worn out from play, play, play. Sometimes I refer to her as The Dog That Ate My Life because so many of my other interests have paled compared to chasing the ball around the house.

We still miss Justin and there are times when I find tears trickling out. I made peace with the pain by thinking that the feeling in my heart was it cracking open wide enough for Justin to move in there to live with me always. I remember the day we put his ashes in my parents' backyard alongside Tiny's grave and those of other family dogs from over the years. Cycles turn. Love isn't lost, it's transmuted. I believe Justin would have been offended if we could have managed to live without a dog. Fiona doesn't take his place—she's her own sweet self. In a dozen years or so, we'll have to cope with it all over again. But it's worth it. Loss is inevitable and that's why it's so important to love as much as possible while we can. That's true for dogs, for people, even places.

Even Enos Park.

(December 1996)

Finnegan

"I probably shouldn't tell you this," said Kevin with some trepidation, "but our neighbor Suzy told me there's a stray standard poodle running around in Rochester." So it begins.

We'd talked about getting another poodle to keep Fiona company so I followed up with Suzy and traced the dog to the Rochester police department, then to the pound. The Sangamon County Animal Control Shelter has a thankless task since they round up stray animals plus owners drop off unwanted pets. No matter how full the cages are, the tide of fur simply doesn't stop. It keeps rolling in and only one out of four animals goes back out the front door. I knew that as I walked past the pens looking for #48. I kept apologizing to the others, "I'd like to take you all home, really I would, but I can't."

Horrendous though it was to deal with the hundreds of pleading eyes, I can point to a record of having given homes to five cats and three dogs over a span of 20 years, all adopted from shelters. It's not as much as I'd like to do, but it's as much as I've been able to do without becoming overwhelmed. (For example, Kevin knew someone who brought so many animals into her house that it was no longer fit for human habitation. I'll spare you the details.)

When I found #48, he was indeed a black standard poodle but what a pathetic sight! His fur was matted and so long it covered his eyes. I wanted to take him home right then but the folks at the pound said he wouldn't be available for adoption until after 2:00 the next day, because their policy is to give owners a three-day period to claim their pets. That's reasonable. "The first person who's here at 2:05 tomorrow for him will get him," the woman at the desk told me.

Tuesday I was at the pound's door at 9:15 before they opened. I plopped down in a chair and simply waited, well ahead of the hordes of people I imagined would be vying for the dog. I daresay the shelter workers had a good chuckle over that. I watched the parade of animals go in and only one go out to a new home. Periodically I'd walk back to tell the doggy that I'd have him bailed out soon.

At promptly 2:05, the papers were signed and I finally got to check that there really were eyes under that matted mess. He was more than happy to hop into the car with me and happier still when the first stop was at a groomer's to get the hair shaved off his face so he could see again. Then he got an ice cream from Dairy Queen. When we picked Kevin up from work, I was no longer plain old Lola, I had become Lola, Goddess-Empress of the Universe. It was glorious—I hadn't had a male react that way to me since I lured Kevin with imported beer when we were first dating.

The rest of the evening was spent cutting the burrs out of his coat and washing the filth off of him. He seemed dazed but pleased to discover a beautiful white fluffy poodle at the house. Friday he visited Dr. Paul McGowan who said he was in basically good shape but severely malnourished, tilting the scales at only 47 pounds when he should weigh about 70. When he was shaved to the skin, it revealed sharp ribs and hip bones. People actually asked if he was part greyhound.

What to name him? Kevin liked Prince Rupert of the Rhine, in honor of the first man on record with an authenticated poodle, Boy. (Rupert's enemies accused Boy of witchcraft, claiming that no dog could possibly be that smart without being in league with the Devil. He died at the battle of Marsten Moor in 1644.) I figured that I'd named Fiona so Kevin could decide on this one and for a while, it was looking like Jock Pierre would win out. Then 'Finnegan' was proposed and Kevin liked the idea of "Prince Rupert of the Rhine, known to his drinking buddies as Finnegan."

Is it easy rescuing and rehabilitating a dog? No, of course not. But Finnegan is worth it. The adoration in his eyes reminds us that we hold a sacred trust to care for him and protect him. We have much the same feeling about houses, neighborhoods and communities. Destruction is easy—it's preservation that takes effort. And it's preservation which feels the most rewarding to know we've saved something that others would have thrown away. I suspect that as we all continue to work on Enos Park, we'll find love returned there, too.

(June 1997)

~LOLA'S WORLD~

Updating a Look

When I met her in my 20's, it was a casual friendship, sort of a lark to hang out with her. Over the next two decades, I'd drop in to visit her when the mood struck but then, in the last few years, I found I needed her. I began to feel panicky without her. Then it dawned on me—she was really harming more than helping and I had to cut her off.

I refer, of course, to Lady Clairol.

As my mother would drive me to nursery school, she'd tell me how my father's side of the family had beautiful black hair and one day mine would be like theirs. She referred to her own as "dishwater blonde" but to me it looked lovely, brown with golden highlights like mine. She wore a page-boy style, held firmly by a rat (no, not that kind—a stuffed tube of netting with the hair rolled over then anchored with bobby pins). Mine cascaded down to my waist until the fateful day when I gave myself a crew cut to look more like Elvis Presley. My poor mother sobbed all night.

But as I reached my teenage years, it became obvious that it wasn't going to turn color on its own and it would have to be helped along. I never tried it during high school because I had the example of "Plastic Erin" before me—a girl in my class whose black dye had turned her hair green, leaving her open to endless jokes on any day except St. Patrick's. I think I was out of college before I bought my first bottle of Clairol Loving Care and went from sunny brown to raven. I liked the dark, mysterious look and, after a few shampoos, it would gradually wash out.

It was Dave Barry who caused me to stop and re-examine my ways last year. He made some crack in his column about aging women always having only two flat, fake-looking dyes on their hair, black or orange, both Halloween colors. (He neglected to mention straw yellow bleached hair like the hay bales beneath the pumpkins and witches' hats.) I'd seen my share of shoe polish black-haired women and anxiously looked at my own locks where color had concentrated beyond any hope of washing out. I had roots showing and a growing collection of silver strands to go with them. I was desperate. The $8 clip joints I was going to weren't helping matters, either. Too often, my mother would ask, "Oh, did you cut your own hair?"

In a roundabout way, it was Fiona who saved me. She and Kevin were walking in the park when a woman with two black standard poodles saw them and wandered over to chat. As I've mentioned, poodle parents are as bad as VW bug drivers for immediately gravitating toward each other. Their owner, Cathy, has a hair salon and I began going there. She embarked on a long-term process to get rid of the flat black in my hair, replacing it with a more natural dark brown with charcoal highlights.

It's true that I'll never look 21 again and anyone who cards me does so as a bit of playful gallantry. As I get older, it takes more work, more time, more money for upkeep. Staying even becomes a goal in and of itself. Drink more water. Eat better. Deliberately park farther away. Find reasons to go up and down stairs instead of cunningly consolidating trips (and stupidly accumulating fat). I bought a few dresses at Land's End in brighter colors than I usually wear, coral and turquoise, to welcome spring and I've tried some new colognes. With a devil-may-care attitude, I think, what the heck, I'm worth it!

It's all paying off, too. I find I feel more confident, more successful, more willing to start conversations and reach out to people. The positive energy I've spent on this fix-up project is continuing to radiate. It works just the same way with Enos Park. The more paint and flowers and clean up we do, the more likely we are to spill over into positive feelings about our homes and our neighbors. We build community as we polish our best features. Excitement is every bit as contagious as despair and it's a *lot* more fun!

Be part of the excitement. As we rededicate Enos Park and work on the Competitive Communities Initiative, we've got a chance to make it a "field of dreams" six blocks square.

(May 1997)

Procrastination

Well, the good news is that I don't look like a chipmunk and I still get to use my favorite Garfield glow-in-the-dark toothbrush.

Let's back up a little. I avoid potentially painful events with remarkable creativity, such as the string of at least six different excuses over a two-year period to reschedule my oral surgery. Several dentists had said I really needed to get my wisdom teeth out because the upper ones had come in at an angle. True, when I sneezed, I'd bite the inside of my cheeks but I was still reluctant to part with any of my 32 pearlies. After all, isn't the idiom "it's like pulling teeth" used to show how difficult something is? I had visions of dentistry done in the Old West by barbers with pliers brandishing bottles of whiskey for anesthetic. "Oh, it's not that bad," scoffed my dentist while friends gleefully recounted dry sockets, tangled roots, hospital stays and worse.

I finally steeled myself and made a decision to go through with it a few days ago. I was surprised when the oral surgeon gave me the option of keeping the lower two wisdom teeth and frankly, I seized upon it fervently with promises to keep them squeaky clean (that's where my Garfield child-size toothbrush comes in). He kept calling nitrous oxide "happy gas" which amused me almost as much as the way he and his staff told me earnestly to "believe in myself" as though I were competing in the Olympics instead of the Dental Chair Rally. These clearly were professionals used to dealing with nervous patients who might bolt: if a technician had come in dressed as Barney to hold my hand and sing, "I love you, you love me" as I went under, it wouldn't have surprised me in the slightest.

What did amaze me was waking up groggily a few minutes later and finding that it wasn't particularly painful. In fact, I was back on solid food that evening with no swelling, no discoloration, no chipmunk face at all.

And I felt darn silly for the years of avoiding something that turned out not to be a big deal at all.

I've been on a binge of cleaning up other things I've procrastinated on, too. We recently had a locksmith in and for $45 fixed problems which had bothered us for nearly three years. We repaired the handrail on the front steps where it had rusted away to a liability suit waiting to happen. I finally found some bookcases with reinforced shelves which hopefully will not bow under the weight of so many books—I bought them, got them delivered and assembled and I'm now loading stacks onto them. We installed a rack in the hall so that brooms don't fall over and startle us or the pets. We got the living room rug cleaned and had the internal leak in the refrigerator repaired. Kitchen cabinets have been straightened so that things neither lurk in the dark nor leap out when the door is opened. I bought wicker baskets to hold papers that had been stacking up on the desk. Even so, it's a constant battle to hold our own and there are many more items waiting for attention. As I'm fond of saying, every house is a case study in entropy, where what's organized devolves into disorganization. As energy runs down, the sun itself will eventually burn out like the bulb on our porch light. Yup, all that and my cleaning service quit so the dust bunnies are my problem again.

Yet each thing we get done removes another bit of nagging guilt. I suspect almost everyone has something to fret about around the house—a drippy faucet, a slow drain, a piece of trim to put back, a chore around the yard, whatever, we all have them. The question is whether we give in to entropy or if we take charge, take control. As the Enos Park Neighborhood Improvement Association motto declares, "If we don't put effort into creating what we want, we must then put effort into coping with what we have." Why endure what can be changed? And with neighbors like ours in EPNIA, there's a hand to help and a smile that will light when we work together. Procrastinating adds to stress; the relief of doing what needs to be done is a sometimes surprising joy.

(September 1997)

Computers and Classes

Along the roadside are stands with pumpkins and scarecrows propped on hay bales. The wheel of the year has turned again to autumn which for me is the fall training season. I crisscross Illinois to show educators how to use state-produced career information software. Yet in the midst of scenic beauty, I re-discover an ugly truth: when it comes to computers, Murphy was an optimist.

"Everything that can go wrong will go wrong" seems woefully inadequate to describe the myriad ways that a room full of networked computers can balk at the worst moment. With six years of experience, I've developed a sort of Zen serenity in the face of disaster. Sometimes files lock, error messages dance tauntingly on the screen, projection equipment goes belly up. I take plenty of paper materials so that we can cover essential points even if the technology flops. I've become adept at verbal tap-dancing so that groups can be trained whether or not Murphy strikes.

At the end of a day, I sometimes feel like I've been dragged over several miles of rough road after hours of alligator wrestling. What makes it worthwhile is that I'm doing what I'm designed for. I used to work directly with displaced workers plus clients in my private practice. I don't doubt that I had quite an impact on some people's lives. Nonetheless, I burned out badly after being the only outplacement counselor at the McDonnell Douglas center when they laid off 4,000 workers in four months. Sometimes I'd go out to my car, roll up the windows and scream until I was ready to face the next group of frightened, angry people who poured in my office. Merely speaking for a few hours at a time to guidance counselors, teachers, administrators and agency personnel is no big deal by comparison. More importantly, I can train them to use career information to help the students and adults they serve. This allows me to leverage what

I know to reach many thousands of people instead of just the few I can see myself.

Best of all is teaching part-time at the University of Illinois at Springfield. My undergrad and graduate students are working adults, typically counselors in the Illinois Employment and Training Centers. They're alert and eager, passionate about finding ways to help their clients move from welfare to work, or from unemployment back to a job. None of them fits the stereotype of paper pushing bureaucrat. (Presumably, those folks remain at the office while my students come to the Career Development Specialist program to earn their certificates.)

In training, I want participants to leave the workshop able to use the software. But in my class, I have months to inspire students with what I hope will be a lifelong sense of wonder about all the resources available to them. "Understanding and Utilizing Career and Labor Market Information" (I'm innocent! I didn't name it!) may sound dry as dust, but to me it's a topic alive with intrigue and possibilities. By the end, I want them to realize that we live in an ocean of information and that they can find exactly what they and their clients need to surf the waves of change. It's not just statistics and demographics and projections: labor market information can be something as hilarious and horrifying as the film *Roger & Me* that I show to each class.

If I hadn't gone into career development, urban planning, adaptive reuse and historic preservation might have been attractive fields. Fond as I am of the past, my real focus is on the future and the power we have to create the reality we choose. It's both true of careers and true of our work to return Enos Park to one of the most desirable neighborhoods in Springfield. Hey, being an EPNIA volunteer isn't just a job—it's an adventure! Theodore Roosevelt said, "The best reward life has to offer is the opportunity to work hard at work worth doing." Enos Park offers any number of ways to put your skills and time to use at work which is well worth doing, indeed.

(October 1997)

Career Fairs

What's worse: competing with Harriet Tubman, come back from the grave, or a two-headed fetal pig? Maybe that's not part of your job, but it is mine.

I'm a trainer for the Illinois Department of Employment Security and so I was recently invited to be a guest speaker at a local grade school. I was informed that I had a tough act to follow since the day before a lady portraying Harriet Tubman of Underground Railway fame had been there. The kindergartners hadn't quite grasped that she wasn't the real deal. "Play acting" is a tenuous concept compared to a living, breathing woman describing her experiences during the Civil War era. My message about modern day careers was pretty bland by comparison.

Usually I enjoy public speaking—give me a wireless microphone and I'll cheerfully plunge into a crowd to talk for an hour without notes. No problem. This time, however, I was nervous. What I know about six-year-olds would fit neatly into a thimble with room left over. (Truth to tell, my only experience is having been six myself once upon a time.) I spent days and days over-preparing, contingency planning and trying to plot ways to keep kids' attention while discussing the value of education and career planning. When my audience filed into the room, none taller than my waist, I was coping with sweaty palms that I don't get standing in front of a whole auditorium filled with adults.

To add to the fun, I'd been told the children were going on a field trip to the Dana Thomas House the next day so I'd designed my handouts around careers in architecture and construction. I had a short biography of Frank Lloyd Wright prepared plus pictures of houses from around the world. Well, no, they weren't going there after all. Oops. With 30 kids K-2 it turned out I didn't have enough clay and toothpicks for them all to do a project, either. It's said that no battle plan survives first contact with the enemy—how many teaching plans get scuppered just as fast? Mine sure did.

Kids are a tough audience because they're obvious about it when something doesn't engage them. I quickly discovered they didn't like being read to from a book and they yelled out when they couldn't see the card I held up of a dinosaur at a drafting table. (Dino Cards get around race and gender issues by showing stegosaurus dentists, brontosaurus receptionists, etc.) However, they did pay close attention when I was telling them about my own life and how I'd blundered around before finding my calling. I didn't get to use the story of Frank Lloyd Wolf huffing and puffing and blowing down houses of sticks and straw, but they understood the Goldilocks idea of trying out careers until there's a right fit. Looking into their bright upturned faces I wondered if any would remember me telling them to hold out for what they enjoy doing in life. I hope so.

Next I spoke with a dozen kids in grades 4–6. That was easier because they could read and write so my handouts were far more useful. We talked about what they might want to be when they grew up. (I revealed to them that usually when adults ask them that question, they're wondering what they might want to do themselves. They truly *are* trying to get a clue.) Many of the girls wanted to be pediatricians and I had to explain to one that her distaste for science wasn't matching up with her goal. Then I mentioned anatomy class and found we'd suddenly changed to lots of kids who wanted to be lawyers. They seemed focused on salaries but that's typical for children and adults both. I made sure they got the key point and had them repeat "The more you learn, the more you earn." If money's the goal, education's the ticket.

Oh, the two-headed pig? That was in a jar on the table next to mine at a career fair for area high school students this spring. How was I to compete with that? Teens flocked to the other exhibitor's microscope, autopsy photos and basket of chocolates while I offered brochures. I learned my lesson. Maybe next year maybe I'll dress as Dolly Madison and hand out pastries along with career advice. What the heck. Life's much too important to be taken seriously!

(August 2003)

Renovation and Restoration

For me, "rehab" typically brings to mind buildings. Little did I know I was about to embark on a restoration project of a different sort.

Pain is a guest with no manners. It takes up residence and refuses to leave. It keeps one awake at night with loud banging and rides along, uninvited, to each daily activity. Then it has its cousin move in, too; Worry whispers in your ear, "Maybe the pain will get even worse. Maybe a time will come when you won't be able to get up stairs by yourself. Maybe…" then it goes on to list possibilities, each more frightening than the last.

But I got lucky. I fell and hurt my foot and thought it was broken. As it turns out, it wasn't, but in the meantime, I got a referral to an orthopedic specialist and told him about the pain in my left shoulder. He sent me to physical therapy at Springfield Clinic and I began a round of ice packs, ultrasound and exercises. Push against walls, swing a cane in arcs, and pull on latex bands that smell like balloons and, promised my wonderful therapist Diane, I could look forward eventually to strengthening the shoulder muscles. That will end the bone rubbing in the wrong place on a tendon and pain can be evicted at long last.

I'm not the athletic type, but the idea of getting out from under a load of agony is a great motivator. I discovered reserves of willpower which amaze me—I actually do the exercises each day. I tied a length of red stretchy band to my front door where it'd be impossible to miss. (And if visitors should happen to ask about it, I plan to look 'em in the eye and tell them it's the latest decorating trend. Watch HGTV and you'll see odder things.)

I asked Diane how my shoulder had ever gotten into such shape, and she said it's an increasingly common problem. Like carpal tunnel syndrome, it's an occupational hazard of desk work at a keyboard. I knew I'd been in a slump, but she said that expressing it physically pushes bones, muscles and tendons off-kilter. One of my exercises is to sit straight, head up, shoulders back. An interesting side effect is that I feel so much better psychologically when I do. Maybe it's really true that good posture keeps the lungs and other internal organs working better. Then I began to wonder—how many other ideas from my fourth grade health book might be right?

Lately Kevin and I have also been meeting with a registered dietitian to learn more about applied nutrition. She's given us a lot of useful tips, such as how to get around The Great American Clean Plate Syndrome (use a salad plate at home and get a to-go box delivered with restaurant meals, then remove half the super-sized portion before starting.) In writing down everything we eat, we saw patterns that could easily be changed, making a big difference within a few weeks. By working together, Kevin and I are creating new habits which substantially improve our lives. Extra pounds are coming off but more importantly, we feel like we're back in charge of our lives.

Renovation, rehabilitation, restoration and preservation are all words that carry a lot of magic. In Enos Park, we can look around at what's already been accomplished and take pride. Some property owners may still be in a slump, but for the ones who are awake, revitalization is the hot news. Trash gets picked up, yards are tended, houses are painted. Under Marsha Leckrone's leadership this year, ambitious projects have been put in motion. A neighborhood in decline lives with Gloom and Despair perched on the shoulders, muttering, "It can't be done, why bother to try?" Enos Park is on the upswing, and it's like a trumpet call of hope to hear all the plans being made.

What I've learned personally also applies to our community: why settle for pain when joy can be found in taking action?

(August 2001)

Recovery

Surgery has such a way of changing one's perspective. For a while there, the item I most longed for, coveted, dreamed of, and finally *demanded* was ice chips. They seemed ravishingly delightful when I finally got them. Similarly, getting to the bathroom all by myself became a major triumph, a cause for celebration. Sit up in a chair? Brush my hair and put on makeup? Amazing!

Granted, the 90's have given us the term "drive-by surgery" and I was out of St. John's within three days. I would've been climbing the corridor walls if I'd been forced to stay much longer and before HMO's, it could have been a 10-day confinement. Anyone who knows me is aware that I am not good at staying put. It started young—running wild in the aisles at movie theaters, wandering off in dime stores. I was just lucky I grew up and found a job that pays me for driving around and exploring the world. "If you really want me to stay still and recuperate at home," I told my doctor, "perhaps a heavy duty sedative would be in order."

As it was, I spent the first two weeks at home with my mother, my blessed mother, staying with us to help out. I was profoundly grateful for having my mommy when I needed her. I joked, "She cooks, she cleans, she does laundry and even speaks fluent English!" But aside from delicious, nutritious meals—*truly* just like mother used to make—the best part was getting to spend time with her. We hadn't done that since seven years ago when I was getting my house in St. Louis ready to sell. Back then, we both scrubbed and sweated through the hot June days until we had the house scrupulously clean for its new owners. (I also left a bottle of champagne for them on the kitchen counter and a card welcoming them to the house I'd loved for 14 years.)

Time. Nobody has enough. MasterCard did a survey and asked what people most wish they could buy and time topped the list. We all get the same 24 hours, but the question is how to spend those minutes. So many can feel stolen from us by circumstances that we're weary and we hoard the few precious ones of peace and privacy. Time is a gift to be given these days, not an endless stream. And according to an article I read recently, it isn't your imagination: time really does speed up as we age, until the seasons whirl past. Supposedly, it's a function of the dopamine levels in the brain, not just the differences in responsibilities that we have as adults.

We talk about "quality time" with children or parents or friends. The two weeks with my mother reminded me that long, meandering hours of nothing much spent together are the real jewels of existence.

(October 1998)

Magazines

Marley's ghost rattled around with the chains he'd forged during his misspent life, links of metal moneyboxes. I have a suspicion that I'll be trailed by cardboard boxes filled with books, magazines and newspaper clippings—toward the end, some of unopened software, too. Yet oddly enough, for all the paper I've collected, some of the items which have had the most impact on my life have been in magazines picked up in waiting rooms.

It was about a decade ago in St. Louis when I was at a vet's office with a margarine container instead of an animal (don't ask: you'll be happier not knowing the contents). I idly looked through a *Smithsonian* issue and in the back was a small ad for a shop in San Francisco called The Light Opera Gallery, purveyors of Russian lacquered boxes, elaborate perfume bottles and kaleidoscopes. At the time, I owned one 'scope and I wasn't even savvy enough to know that what I had was a teleidoscope with mirrors to make patterns of whatever you point it at instead of using tumbling bits of colored glass. What a scrumptious feast for the senses their catalog was when it arrived! I was dazzled by the array of 'scopes with all types of inner images and outer appearances. Sir David Brewster of Scotland had invented them in the 18th century and coined "kaleidoscope" which comes from Greek words meaning "beautiful to see." I've always been most interested in the image inside and some $10 kaleidoscopes are more appealing than ones costing thousands of dollars. Thus, what started as an ad seen by chance turned into a collection that was even featured in the *State Journal-Register* after I moved to Springfield. (Kevin likes to tease me by telling people that the brass display case for them was custom-made but the truth is, I got it on clearance at Kmart.) My favorite remains my Dragon Scope with over a hundred tiny pieces of stained glass in each of the two rotating wheels.

Another time, I was reading at a doctor's office about careers in the field of recruiting personnel, or headhunting as it's called in the trade. The description of a successful recruiter sounded like me at my best: resourceful, creative in tracking information, and then persuading people into a course of action. I joined a retained executive search firm and actually got paid to hang out at the Washington University business library. The downside was that after a while it seemed like phone soliciting: "Hello, do you happen to know of anyone who'd be interested in a position as a CEO at a leading technology company based in Minneapolis? You would? What a quaint coincidence! Could you fax your resume to me?" Over time, I discovered that the job was a good fit for me in some ways, but working for a tiny company with four people in the office was too close for comfort.

In the late 80's, I was waiting to have my teeth cleaned when I picked up a copy of *Newsweek* and read about the coming thing in software called hypertext. It described a mind-boggling new format where you could have photos, video and audio clips and underlined text which when you clicked on it would take you to related topics. Big deal, you snort—that's just multimedia, like virtually all CD-ROMs. But back then, the world was ruled by DOS and even games were white text on a black screen. What a magazine article described was a quantum leap ahead in presenting information. Would it surprise you to find that I eventually got into multimedia design as part of my job with the state? No, I didn't think so.

Kevin's waiting room experience at our vet's was finding a breeder's ad for Norwegian Lundehunds in a recent issue of *Dog Fancy*. They're three-toed beasties who are double-jointed, the better to climb rocks to hunt birds called puffins. Lundehunds are described as completely non-aggressive toward humans or other dogs and my husband is now convinced that we need one. I'm still dubious. We are, however, waiting to put into practice something we saw in the *Wall Street Journal* on how to buy a castle in Scotland. (Incidentally, in Scotland it's assumed that anyone who buys a castle is, by definition, an American.)

For me, items read by chance turned into a pleasurable hobby, a lucrative job and a marketable skill. Perhaps one day you'll read something in the Enos Park *Banner* such as a quote, a decorating or gardening tip, or a call to volunteering that will change your life when you respond. Be alert for new ideas—you never know when inspiration will strike!

(April 1998)

Golden Shadow

Actually, it was Marianne Williamson who wrote the quote which follows, though it's often ascribed to Nelson Mandela because he used it in his 1994 inaugural speech:

> *"Our greatest fear is not that we are inadequate. Our deepest fear is that we are powerful beyond measure. It is our light, not our darkness, that most frightens us. We ask ourselves, 'Who am I to be brilliant, gorgeous, talented, fabulous?'*
>
> *"Actually, who are you not to be? You are a child of God. Your playing small doesn't serve the world. There's nothing enlightening about shrinking so that other people won't feel insecure around you.*
>
> *"We were born to make manifest the glory of God that is within us. It's not just in some of us; it's in everyone. And as we let our own light shine, we unconsciously give other people permission to do the same. As we are liberated from our own fear, our presence automatically liberates others."*

In essence, Williamson was describing something that's termed the golden shadow. Yes, we're all more intimately familiar with its opposite, the dark shadow that lives within each of us, the aspects we're not proud of, our sources of guilt and shame. Everyone's got 'em if they've been raised by humans (though I'm not taking any bets on children weaned by wolves). To be able to live in society means suppressing our impulses—the part that would go face down into a birthday cake and leave none for the other kids at the party, for example. Knowing that it's wrong to lie, cheat or steal doesn't keep people from occasionally having the desire to do so, but then we push those feelings back down.

The golden shadow, though, is a part we suppress because we're raised "not to blow our own horns," to be modest, to focus on our defects instead of our magnificence. There is very real peer pressure to conform to the status quo. I've read that if crabs are put into a box, they'll sometimes clump in a corner until one can climb over their backs toward the top. Just as it's about to go free, the other crabs will grasp it and drag it back down into the box. Only as I write this now does it occur to me that perhaps they're trying to save their comrade from falling over the edge of the world as they know it. Well-meaning or not, they all stay captive.

I've met an Enos Park crab or two, people who invest their energy into saying that nothing can be done, the neighborhood isn't worth saving, it's too much work, and so on. I don't think they're mean, but I do think they're shortsighted. What if, instead, we focus on what's truly golden about Enos Park? What if we treasure the historic houses, bask in the warmth of knowing even the most modest dwelling may be filled with a loving family? What about the trees as they leaf out this spring dazzle us with the miracle of their renewed greenery? And what is it about Enos Park that's so good that we don't even recognize it because it's under our collective noses?

At Enos Park Neighborhood Improvement Association meetings I look around and believe me, the room is filled with brilliant, gorgeous, talented, fabulous people. As Gail Sheehy wrote in *New Passages*, "The source of continuing aliveness is to find your passion and pursue it with whole heart and single mind." Here's my challenge to you: find more ways to be whole-heartedly enthusiastic about where you live. Take the risk of admitting just how good our neighborhood is—and will be.

(February 2002)

Costumes

So there I was on a September Saturday, walking down the church aisle toward the altar. Fortunately, it wasn't my wedding (I've bagged my limit, thank you very much) but it was my very first experience of being part of traditional nuptials. A matron's dress—does that make you think of gray cotton shirtwaists, cunningly accessorized with thick shoes and a truncheon? Does me. If good weather on a wedding day is supposed to be an omen for happiness, what about three women agreeing enthusiastically on the same pattern and the same fabric? And then finding a seamstress who did very good work for insanely reasonable prices and got the dresses done on time? I had an obligatory spasm of worrying that I looked like an elephant swaddled in maroon drapery but the compliments were frequent and sounded surprised enough to indicate real sincerity. My co-matron of honor Kathy and I made it through Christa's wedding and reception with decorum, even though the necklines had an alarming tendency to try to head south.

It got me to thinking about the role of clothing in our lives. It's not just a matter of matching dresses for wedding pictures; often we're asked/required/coerced into wearing uniforms of one sort or another. Kevin had his share as a sailor, with dungarees and blue shirts when he was in the submarine service. For a while after he began as a computer consultant, his uniform was dress shirts and a tie, except on the casual Friday. He's a jeans kind of guy and he was happy indeed when the ties were dropped for anything other than special meetings.

As for me, I wore white cotton lab smocks and pants for years then graduated to lab coats for a desk job at Mallinckrodt, a chemical company in St. Louis. What with safety glasses, steel-toed shoes and paper hats to keep hair out of the pharmaceutical products, it was no wonder that the running joke was always, "I didn't recognize you with clothes on!" That's what we'd say when we'd run into coworkers out at the mall. Because it was typically covered up, hair became quite fascinating and alluring, I suppose that's just human nature. Later when I was working at a government project to help laid-off workers, we didn't have uniforms but I made a point of never wearing black to work. My theory was that my clients were already in mourning for their lost jobs and for a way of life that had vanished with a proverbial pink slip.

If uniforms serve to remind us of purpose and cohesion to group values and identity, then what is Halloween except the exact opposite? It's wild individuality, a chance to be authentic in a way that isn't socially acceptable the other 364 days of the year—I'm thinking of a high school pal whose costume revealed he was more than casually interested in dressing as a woman. His shaved legs were something of a tip-off, as well as his expertise in walking in heels.

My own costumes over the years have been varied, some so close to reality that people asked why I didn't bother to dress up (tarot card reader) to ones where I wasn't recognizable. Let's see, there was Sassafras, ditzy flower child hippie chick, Gina Venturini, Mafia princess, January, swashbuckling swordswoman, and Brandy in a bleached blonde wig and red miniskirt who tended to lean on lamp posts, if you get my drift. Best of all was Margot the Infested. For a year I belonged to the Society for Creative Anachronism, the medieval re-creation group, and their annual Changelings banquet was a sort of come-as-you-aren't party. I showed up in the shabbiest wig I could find, shuffling in burlap rags I'd artfully aged in the bottom of a garbage can and rolled in fireplace ashes. I'd grunt and shove a wooden bowl at people until they gave, just to get me to move downwind. Hey, I made $3.62 that night!

Do clothes truly make the man? No, but they help get a certain impression across. Appearances count because they create perceptions which can become realities as a result of self-fulfilling prophecies. We want Enos Park to be uniformly beautiful and well-tended but I also hope for the flair and individuality of costumes. Dress up your house for autumn, for Halloween, and for the winter holidays. Let your self-expression show all the way to the curb!

(October 2002)

Trike

Time to get out the virtual champagne to celebrate! I cycled all the way around Washington Park for the first time, a full circuit. I had planned my strategy during the winter: go east on Williams, use the sidewalk at Mac-Arthur, then west on Williams on the other side of the park boulevard, around the loop near South Grand Avenue West and then down the notorious hill and back to my starting point. Go clockwise and use gravity instead of fighting the slope—and it worked! All I had to do was ignore a couple of pesky "One Way Do Not Enter" signs.

Oh, there were hills but I managed. 2.5 miles might not seem like much in the grand scheme of things but it was a major accomplishment for me. Better still, I rode all the way up Lincoln when that very evening I'd been thinking, "Well, I'll always have to walk up that final hill." Being wrong turned out to be a pleasure this time. Previously I hadn't gotten more than a quarter of the way up but I just kept going, then reached a place where I thought, "I will *not* give up and walk it at this point." What an endorphin rush! It didn't matter that there wasn't a soundtrack, I had my own with blood singing in my ears and my heart pounding double time. It was somewhere well beyond glorious.

I remember when Kevin got involved with the Springfield Bike Club and he'd invite me to join them for events after the rides. No, I said, I wouldn't have anything in common with "those people." I suppose I thought they were all Olympic contenders who'd talk of nothing but gears, sprockets and training regimes. Wrong, wrong indeed. Their unofficial motto is, "An eating club with a biking problem." Turned out they were some of the nicest folks I've ever met. Once I started hanging around with them, it wasn't long until they began encouraging me to ride, too. That's the insidious part of peer pressure, good or ill, we tend to take up what those around us are doing.

I did lots of research on the Internet to find adult tricycles because I'd never learned to ride a bike without training wheels. Finally I narrowed it down to two contenders, a Lightfoot Trilobike and a Haluzak Triumf. The Bike Rack in St. Charles ordered in the Trilobike for me to test ride and they also had a Penninger Voyager and a Triumf in stock. It was so Goldilocks: one too heavy, one too light, but the Triumf was just right. Taking off on it felt like *freedom*.

My beloved Silver was sent from the factory last fall and friends helped assemble her on our front porch. (No, I never, ever say "Hi ho Silver and away!" Don't ask why, I just don't.) Cycling in Washington Park at first was a 'bug in the bowl' experience because I'd ride as far as possible in one direction, then go back the other way until another hill stopped me. My ambition was modest, just to make it through a ride without any kind person offering to help me with a push up an incline. Nowadays when teenage boys zooming past yell, "Cool!" am I vain enough to enjoy it? Why yes, as a matter of fact, I am.

This spring, I continued my assault on the hill on the south side of the park, just over the lagoon bridge. It's one that even serious cyclists discuss but a trike has an advantage when it comes to slow plugging up a slope—it's possible to crank, brake, crank and inch forward. It's not elegant, but it works. Having gotten up the steepest grade, there's still a series of slopes past there. I've now done nearly five miles and while I haven't felt the same giddy delight since conquering that first hill, I remain grateful for the enthusiastic support of friends who've helped me celebrate each new achievement.

One can have great triumphs on a small scale: skip the Tour de France, I'm blitheringly happy to have made a single circuit. Cycling through the leafy green park as the sun slanted through the trees in a golden haze felt like a lucid dream. All the work I put in on the exercycle over the winter paid off. And so it is with Enos Park. We put in the work and discover that the efforts yield returns beyond what we would have ever dared to dream.

(July 2002)

Legacies

It's interesting, the legacies that people leave behind them.

If I checked the abstract or other historical documents, I could find the name of the fellow I curse, sometimes several times a day. He was a developer in Springfield a century ago who platted my neighborhood. He figured out that by squeezing the houses closer together, he could get an extra lot on the block and sell another house. The profit that lined his pockets was quickly spent and he himself is long dust. Yet day after day I back down a shared driveway and remember him unkindly. Other residents on the block feel the same: his short-term gain has now led to inconvenience and aggravation for the people who bought his houses for a hundred years. My next door neighbors are great people to share a driveway with—if one is going to be forced to share—and that only makes me feel worse when I knock their rain spout off yet again. (Once I backed into their barrel planted with flowers. Becky was very nice about it and said they were at the end of their season anyway.) I don't know what sort of afterlife that developer believed in but personally, I don't care if it's hot or cold, I just hope that wherever he is now, that it's *narrow*.

Quite a different legacy was left by Erma Bombeck. For three decades I chuckled over her trials and tribulations with panty hose, purses, her husband and kids, and life in suburbia. She had a wonderfully wry way of looking at the world and magnifying its absurdities. She kept writing her columns through her fight with both cancer and kidney disease. She refused to use her fame to be put ahead on the waiting list for a transplant and that probably cost her life.

Her readers will all have their favorite columns, many of which have been collected into books. Erma also showed that humor writers can do serious, heart string-pulling columns, so every now and then I'd find tears mixed into my laughter. The one I remember best described how she and her husband were sitting at a picnic table in their backyard. Their kids were grown and had moved away so that once again, it was just the two of them as it had been at the start of their marriage. They were sharing a jar of mixed vegetables and her husband said, "Here, I saved the pickled cauliflower for you because I know you like it." Real love, durable love, turns out to be something quite different than youthful passion. That column taught me to look for love in the small, daily gestures, such as the way Kevin makes coffee for me in the morning.

James Rouse, another person I admire, also passed on recently. In the early 1980's, he had an unexpected delay during his stay in downtown St. Louis. He wandered over to the abandoned hulk of Union Station and stared around the cavernous space. At one end was The Terminal Hotel and with sad irony, that seemed to sum up the building's decline. Trains no longer pulled into the station, they arrived at the little "Am Shack" a few blocks away. But Rouse wasn't an ordinary tourist. He was the man who had coined the term "urban renewal" and he had a record of success in taking inner city properties and turning them around into festival market places, full of kiosks, restaurants and upscale shops. Rouse was responsible for renovations in Boston, Baltimore, Milwaukee, New York City, Atlanta, New Orleans—in fact, *Time* magazine went so far as to say that it was a rare major city that hadn't been "roused." Union Station went from a white elephant to cash cow; it's one of the most visited tourist destinations in St. Louis and it has been revitalized to serve for yet another century. President Clinton said, "He showed us that we can build communities worthy of the character and the optimism of the American people."

Erma Bombeck helped me to think of marriage as wider and deeper than I'd imagined while James Rouse expanded the possibilities of adaptive re-use of historic properties. Unlike that developer who cramped things for generations to come, they made life larger, grander and more full with their vision. It's been a privilege to know them and to carry on, in some small way, their ideas as I write for the *Banner* each month.

(May 1996)

Family History

Remember home movies? Those cumbersome metal cameras whirring away to record family events? Before the films were transferred to video-tape, we used to set up the projection screen, turn off the lights then watch our family history. Sometimes it seemed to consist of flickering between Christmas, dyeing Easter eggs, riding at the amusement park, then the Labor Day barbeque, a Thanksgiving table, then Christmas again. The older I get, the more it seems that life itself is on fast forward.

And so here we are at Back to School season. Shelves are stocked with all that delicious paraphernalia: the newly sharpened pencils, pristine note-book paper, boxes of crayons and fresh book bags. And oh! The scent of new textbooks! I loved burying my nose in them, both literally and figura-tively. School starting was the moment I'd waited for since the tearful end of class in June. (Much to my delight, I discovered summer school in jun-ior high.) For me, it was an opportunity to play with all sorts of dazzling new ideas. I had a family that respected education with the fervor of peo-ple who'd had to work hard for a living in the cotton fields of Arkansas instead of being able to stay in school when they wanted to.

Life has some odd quirks. I owe a lot to a man whose name I'll never know. It was just after the turn of the century when he took the time to tutor my grandfather outside of class hours. Jim had fallen behind because of family responsibilities and he was embarrassed to be a 12-year-old fourth grader or to sit with the smaller kids in the one-room schoolhouse. With the teacher's help, he graduated from eighth grade, quite a respect-able accomplishment in those days.

Jim's daughter Pauline worked in the cotton fields, too, but her parents made sure she graduated from high school. My mother didn't make it to medical school as she might have under different circumstances but what a gift she has for making knowledge come alive! Watching her explore the backyard for mysteries with her grandchildren now reminds me of how she encouraged my sister and me to always be alert for information. It should come as no surprise that Lorna has her doctorate in jurisprudence and I'm lagging along with only two master's degrees because we were taught to enjoy learning. And we both owe it to that teacher who helped our grandfather succeed in school.

What each of us here in Enos Park does may seem insignificant but small efforts snowball over time. What you are doing today, at home, at work, and in our neighborhood may seem very routine and uneventful. Yet it's impossible to gauge the diameter of a ripple from the size of the stone that's thrown into the water and, similarly, your kind word to a neighbor may have an impact far beyond a momentary pleasantry. As you look back in your own life, you'll find many examples where being at the right place at the right time made all the difference in the world. What if you hadn't gone to the Laundromat that day which led to meeting the woman who's become your best friend? Or picked up a book with a phrase that leaped out at you?

It's all woven together in the most wonderful and magical way. If we take the time and make the effort to restore Enos Park to one of the best kept neighborhoods in town, what effect will that have? As we've worked on our own house, we've gotten to know neighbors better and we learned new skills. We gloat over every house on our street that's painted and refurbished and we wave at the people who are outside doing the work. I cannot help but believe that a well-tended house and yard leads to a sense of pride, dignity and more respect for one's self and others.

Of course, the tricky part is that we really don't know what the long term impact will be of all this neighborhood building, any more than that teacher could have imagined that his extra time with one child would have such an effect on generations to come. Sometimes we have to take it on faith and believe that the effort we invest today will have dividends over many tomorrows. Enos Park is worth the investment.

(September 1993)

Packrats

Well, the moving van came Friday and we're down to mopping up the last few items in the basement, storage shed and garage. It was a long and exhausting Labor Day weekend and from the stacks of boxes in the new house, it bodes to be more work for months to come.

How do moves fall apart so fast? I had visions—common, I'm told—of everything coming off with precision: each item sorted, packed, neatly labeled and color coded for the correct room at the new location then stacked tastefully against a wall. That lasted for only a few minutes. After that, it was cram everything into boxes scrounged from Barnes & Noble (bless them!) and the movers soon had the parlor filled with boxes helter skelter, "upstairs bath" on top of "basement" next to "bedroom." The whole thing reminded me of one of those sponge creatures pressed flat that explodes in size when placed in water. All the *schtuff* that had been hidden in closets is now all released into its overwhelming reality.

Our packrat ways became all too clear. It's not just thousands of books, it's mementos going back to early childhood for both of us. If I'd had more time (read: if I'd had the sense to start packing sooner) I could have enjoyed the emotional archeology of going through the boxes in the attic instead of just shoving them towards the stairs. Even though we sorted out hundreds of magazines to take to shops for trade credit, that left hundreds more to hoist. It's true that books are like snowflakes: beautiful individually but a real mess in a crowd.

The essence of the problem is the belief that an item might be useful at some point and the certainty that there's no way to prove that faster than by parting with it. "Oh, there's where that little thingamajig belongs!! Do we have another? Can we get another? Whaddaya mean, they don't make them anymore?!?" That's the paranoid fantasy but must it extend to things as ludicrous as an empty plastic bottle? I managed to pitch quite a few things, sell some and donate others and we plan on a blow-out yard sale as we unpack our hastily grabbed possessions.

See, I put off packing long past the point of reason because I didn't really want to move. Ambivalence led to paralysis. Kevin and I love our wee blue house so it's been terribly hard to let go. Sure, it's the American Dream to move upward to a bigger house and yes, we'd only planned to stay here three to five years but it's wrenching. Enos Park has problems—we all know that. But the neighborhood foot patrols and the way we can come together to meet the challenges is inspiring. I still remember how so many people turned out for the EPNIA meetings to demand changes when needed and how our determination has led to real progress. There are many bright, shining moment when we've reared up on our collective hind legs and said, "We *deserve* better than this and we'll make sure we have it!"

And that's what it takes. "Those who refuse to accept less than the very best," wrote Oscar Wilde, "often find they get it." Let's prove him right.

(September 1994)

COME BE A PART OF THE
SAFETY IN OUR NEIGHBORHOOD

Happiness

Lately I've been studying happiness because so many awful things cross my desk in an average day about the economy, layoffs and the general decline of Western civilization that I need something as a counterbalance. For example, one article claimed a "happiness calculus" can determine how much money it takes to make people blissful. The figure arrived at, $1.5 million dollars, would certainly brighten my day even if it's what falls out of Bill Gates' pockets in the dryer. Nonetheless, I have doubts about money buying happiness. What about all those stories of lottery winners who go bankrupt in a flaming spiral of debt? Then again, maybe they're the newsworthy exceptions while the ones who do well with the money never show up as cautionary tales.

Some psychologists suggest there's a happiness set-point that people will return to after the new wears off on marriages, jobs or windfalls. Abe Lincoln famously said, "Most people are about as happy as they choose to be." Now, I'm not suggesting boot strapping one's self out of clinical depression but rather, making some conscious choices about what we think and how we live.

Too often, being a grown-up becomes a matter of putting one foot before the other blindly to sleepwalk through life. Looking back, several years in my 30's disappeared into a long gray swath of nothingness. Some were spent "with a full glass and an empty heart," as a song lyric goes, while I tried to drown my disappointments. (Alas, as any serious drinker knows, sorrow floats.) I was lucky, I managed to get off alcohol nearly a dozen years ago and it was a substantial lifestyle improvement. Days now are strung along weeks like jewels that sparkle in every imaginable hue. To paraphrase the famous quote about being rich or poor, I've been happy and I've been miserable, and happy is better.

There's a question, too, about what constitutes "enough" happiness. One fellow spent years in therapy until his psychiatrist discharged him, telling him that the flat dullness he felt was normal, congratulations, that's the cure. Wait a minute, he thought, is that all there is? While Thoreau wrote of most people leading lives of quiet desperation, surely that's not the goal to strive for! It's not enough to just escape the dreary doldrums, the human heart wants something more.

Martin Seligman is a psychologist who's addressing that in the new field of Positive Psychology. Its purpose is to maximize strengths and virtues instead of wallowing around in pathology. (You can go to www. authentichappiness.com and try out some of the free surveys to identify your own strengths and compare your level of happiness with others' by gender, education and income level, etc.) Maybe it shouldn't come as any surprise that applying kindness, generosity, courage, humor and optimism to life lead to an improved mood, but there it is. You can use your best strengths by volunteering in EPNIA where there's never, ever a shortage of opportunities.

Seligman also discusses three paths to happiness: the Pleasure Life, the Good Life and the Meaningful Life. If they were places, you might think of Las Vegas as exemplifying the Pleasure Life of fun and sensory stimulation while the Good Life might be a close-knit Illinois farming community built on hard work. We tend to think of the Meaningful Life as places like an inner city mission, but the truth is, you don't need to move to Calcutta in order to be of service—Enos Park is a great place to start, folks. A full life includes elements of all three, so that play, work and purpose blend into a whole.

As we celebrate the 4th of July we can remember that the Declaration of Independence doesn't guarantee happiness, just the right to pursue it. You've still got to catch it and wrestle it to the ground yourself. I like a quote I found from 1869: "The best way to secure future happiness is to be as happy as is rightfully possible today." I don't deny that it's a hard world out there, but I think the best response to it is finding the courage to feel joy.

(July 2003)

Success

"When I hear about people making vast fortunes without doing any productive work or contributing anything to society, my reaction is, 'How do I get in on that?'" Dave Barry's quote always makes me laugh—no moralistic platitudes such as "success only comes before work in the dictionary." I love the sheer audacious *honesty* of it, an exuberant "Awright!" like a three-year-old finding a cookie jar left unguarded.

"Boondoggle" is a Scottish word that came into English and it means an unearned reward. Is that really all it's cracked up to be? I've been in the supposedly enviable position of being paid lots of money for doing hardly anything and it's not as much fun as you might think. For example, I worked at a pharmaceutical plant years ago where the pay and benefits were great, the people were nice, the environment was clean and the job wasn't stressful. I hated it. I'd go out at break time and stroll around the parking lot looking up at the blue sky above, longing to fly beyond the high fences topped with barbed wire. But heck, I wasn't doing time, I was there by choice! All I had to do was walk out the gates and keep on going; plenty of friends had done it. I'd imprisoned myself in a job that wasn't right for me, then fastened the golden handcuffs with credit card debt and a mortgage.

Still, I was covertly digging away a spoonful at a time, tunneling out by changing the way I thought about myself. Truly, "There is only one success—to be able to spend your life your own way." Back then I hid books and magazines on career development in my desk drawer. I'd sneak them out and read them in off moments. I certainly wouldn't have taken them down to the break room and risk getting laughed at by coworkers.

Fast forward two decades and I've been there, done that quite thoroughly as a career consultant. Thousands of people have passed through my life, sharing their hopes, fears and dreams with me. Their stories have been woven into my own memories: a postman who lost his job because he left the soap samples in rural route mailboxes but not the 'occupant' address cards; a woman who'd been abused in foster homes until she finally found a family who loved her; an older man whose stone-hard hands engulfed mine as he tearfully thanked me for helping him find a new direction for his life after the mine shut down. Then there was the surrealism of GM factory workers lined up like kids waiting for a turn on Santa's lap, only it was me they were seeing for three minutes each to revamp their resumes. Often people would claim they couldn't fill in the government paperwork because they'd forgotten their glasses but in fact, they couldn't read. One fellow had zero years of education because he stayed a step ahead of the truancy officer but that bit of cleverness left him completely illiterate. Throwing bricks at rats may have seemed cool on the mean streets but it wasn't translating into marketable job skills. I tried to follow up but his phone was disconnected so I'll always wonder what became of him.

As my day job I now design career development materials and systems, contribute to national websites and train the next generation of career counselors in workshops. I've taught graduate school part-time since 1996 so there are hundreds of former students in Illinois plus a few around the country. Having achieved my dream, what do I have in my desk drawers nowadays? My files are stuffed with house plans I've drawn, not particularly well but with such sincerity—if only that counted as much as ability! To create myself anew would mean acquiring skills and contacts and also once again giving up what's comfortable and familiar.

At present we're wondering what the medical district will mean for our area. We hope it will all be positive and, unlike Dave Barry's quote, we're more than willing to produce something of value and to work hard to get good things the old fashioned way, by earning them. Change is scary, even when it's for the better. We'll have to decide as a community what we want, let go of what's been and choose our direction yet again. And of course we will. With a century and a half under our belts, heavens knows, we've had practice reinventing Enos Park!

(April 2003)

Appendix

~History of Enos Park~

A Short History of Enos Park

Adapted from the Restore Springfield House Tour Booklet

The Connecticut Yankee, Pascal P. Enos, and his wife, Salome, were pioneers in the development of Springfield. In fact, prior to 1823, when President Monroe sent Pascal Enos to establish a land office in the Springfield district, the town was "nearly a scattering of squatters." The Enoses, along with several other early developers (Taylor, Cox and Iles) were responsible for much of the development and design of the city of Springfield. The Enoses owned much land in the area and chose what is now the North Seventh and Enterprise location as the site for their house. This location was even visited by a newly elected President Lincoln in 1860 on the occasion of Julia Enos' wedding to Ozias M. Hatch, who was Secretary of State at the time. The former Enos family home site (now called "Pascal Place") and the park that bears their name still serves as a focal point for this historic area of Springfield.

On 4th Street, Edwards Place is the oldest house in Springfield on its original foundation, built in 1833. Helen and Benjamin Edwards lived in the home from 1843–1909. Abraham Lincoln courted Mary Todd as they sat on a black horsehair sofa. (Since 1913 the Italianate mansion has been owned by the Springfield Art Association which now extends into the adjoining complex, housing an art gallery, school of art, and the Michael Victor II Art Library.)

By the turn of the century, the Enos Park area hosted an economically diverse collection of homes. Alongside the family estates of Springfield area attorneys, physicians and business proprietors, many of Springfield's working class elected to build their homes. Most of these workers were employed by North End manufacturing businesses, including several coal mines, the Illinois Watch Company, the Sangamo Meter Works, the Rolling Mills, the shoe factory, and the railroads.

The Enos Park neighborhood was also ethnically diverse, with Italians, Portuguese, Lithuanians, Polish, Greeks and African Americans. However, the largest group, by far, was the Germans, as the Enos Park area was encompassed by "Goosetown," the German section of town. In the late 1800s, 60% of Springfield residents were German, and most were concentrated in the Goosetown section, drawn by employment at Reisch Brewery or through the skilled trades.

The Enos Park Neighborhood Improvement Association (EPNIA) became involved with the Restore Springfield House Tour because of the historic nature of the neighborhood, the private restoration work taking place in the area, and because of their interest in efforts to stabilize, upgrade and restore the area. Enos Park is a neighborhood in transition. Sprinkled throughout are many single family and duplex restorations that have signaled the beginning of the movement to restore the area and to provide decent housing for its residents. There are wonderful opportunities for spacious homes at an affordable price for the do-it-yourselfer, often with assistance from the Department of Planning and Economic Development.

EPNIA welcomes new members, both people who live in the area and those in Springfield and beyond who have an interest in neighborhood improvement and historic preservation. Call (217) 522-9381 for membership information.

~Acknowledgements~

With Thanks to All

I used to wonder at those long lists of acknowledgements that authors would put in their works—how could so many people have been involved? Obviously, until I knew that, I wasn't ready to publish my own books.

There's a whole study on "the myth of solitary genius." This is nothing as high-flown since really it has more in common with a lot of people tugging on ropes when a mule gets stuck in the mud. It was my family, friends and mentors who got me dragged out of the mire of procrastination. They asked for years, "Hey, when will your book be out?" until it got easier to do it than to explain why it wasn't done.

I also owe the late Sen. Paul Simon a debt of gratitude because I read a quote from him that ran, "People who say they're going to write a book never do." In some ways, it was more helpful to prove him wrong than to believe people telling me they thought I should get published. Ah, the perversities of human nature!

My mother, Pauline Cameron, read to me hour after hour when I was a toddler and gave me my first books to cherish, so yes, she started it all and she's ultimately responsible. She also helped select the columns and proofread the advance copy. My stepfather Hal had been a journalist and he repeatedly urged me to collect my columns into book form so I wish that he were still here to see it. I think my late father, Louis Lucas, would be proud, too.

Jackie Jackson has been a teacher, colleague, friend, mentor, aunt by choice, and role model as an author. She gives me hope for growing into her wisdom, humor and *joie de vivre*. Lately, Jackie has been offering great ideas on this next phase of getting my completed book into readers' hands.

Marilyn Piland adds my column each month to the Enos Park *Banner*. She cajoles columnists, collects material, prints the newsletter, gets it folded, mailed and even has been know to hand deliver it door to door. In a very literal sense, this book wouldn't exist without her efforts since without Marilyn there wouldn't be a newsletter year after year. She also typed the manuscript for this book thus saving me from searching hard drives on six different computers.

Thanks to Diane Wilkes, Doreen Vitkuske, Mary Greer, Joanne Waldman, Rose Jonas, Sandy Costa, Frances Roehm and Jane Goz Goodman for their support and advice. As writers and/or counselors themselves, they helped me to understand the process. Thanks also to Adriel Ippolito and Colleen Quinn for a creating an environment of artistic exuberance at our weekly INFP meetings.

Jim McKee has been kind and encouraging for nearly three decades. He demonstrates that people do voluntarily read poetry and that was enough to get me back into writing it. Actually, my columns are a sideline to what I think of as my real work.

Edward Longcore did a great job of doing the photographs of us, Enos Park and our former home, "The Wee Blue Hoose" on 4th Street.

One always hesitates at this moment: have I forgotten someone? English teachers and professors stroll across my memory, leaving the scent of chalk dust hanging in the air. I remember Richard Gannon at McCluer High School in particular because he was always enthusiastic about my prose and poetry. That helped forge my self-concept as a writer.

The great people who serve on the EPNIA board deserve thanks, as well as all the *Banner* columnists, residents and investors who work on revitalizing Enos Park. Thanks also to readers for their many kind comments over the years. To everyone who has been part of making this book a reality, you have my gratitude.

Most of all, thank you to Kevin Brown for being the best editor I could possibly hope for, with useful suggestions on nearly every column as it rolls off the printer. "Perhaps you'd want to explain this a bit more so the transition is clearer." Huh, really? When it was so clear to me? His perspective as a reader has helped me to be a much better writer than I would be if left to my own devices. His love as a husband lights my world with joy.

~~~~~~

To join the Enos Park Neighborhood Improvement Association

For additional copies of *At Home in the Park: Loving a Neighborhood Back to Life*

Order additional copies from your local bookseller or online at www. iuniverse.com, www.barnesandnoble.com and www.amazon.com. If you're in the Springfield, Illinois area, check the bookstores or better still, join us for EPNIA events! See www.epnia.com for upcoming meetings.

If you'd like to contact me with questions or comments, please email EPNIA@lolalucas.com.

978-0-595-36482-4
0-595-36482-9

www.ingramcontent.com/pod-product-compliance
Lightning Source LLC
Chambersburg PA
CBHW022254290526
45785CB00015B/774